EDWARD DAHLBERG

AMERICAN ISHMAEL OF LETTERS

Selected Critical Essays with an Introduction
by HAROLD BILLINGS

ROGER BEACHAM · PUBLISHER   AUSTIN   1968

FOR BERNICE

PREFACE

EDWARD DAHLBERG's hot love for his art, to use Ford Madox Ford's phrase, is probably without equal in America. It is doubtful that any other writer could be more committed to his work. Though Dahlberg has taught at Black Mountain College, Boston University, Columbia University, the Polytechnic Institute of Brooklyn, New York University, and the University of Missouri at Kansas City, these professorships have been only a means to the end of writing. Dahlberg has been called a brilliant lecturer; but his life remains, in every sense, in his writing. And so to write, and subsist, he has lived chiefly as an eremite, ever wrestling, as he might say, with the angel at Peniel for perception.

After many years of struggle to find publishers, readers, and recognition Dahlberg now, at the age of 67, finds himself with more honor than ever in his career. Jonathan Williams is completing a *Festschrift for Edward Dahlberg* to be published in the summer of 1968; and the fact that seven of Dahlberg's books have been published since 1964 indicates publishers no longer shun him. During 1967 three of his works were reissued in "scholars'" paperback editions. Major literary awards have eluded him, but he has had grants from the Longview Foundation, the National Institute of Arts and Letters, and the Rockefeller Foundation.

The present collection constitutes the first critical work devoted to his writings. Any such collection of critical essays is an Osirian rite for the recollecting and savoring of the whole writer. He is dismembered by the one to be recollected by the many. Echoes of common sight, and sharp notes of individual insight, weave through such a collection to bring into better focus the sometimes blurred and diverse impressions we have of a writer's work.

7

The essays are arranged roughly chronologically according to the date of publication of the Dahlberg work with which each is concerned. Jonathan Williams' essay is presented early because it reviews in depth all of Dahlberg's writing to the publication of *Because I Was Flesh*. The book ends appropriately with Kay Boyle's "A Man in the Wilderness," which not only covers the latest Dahlberg books, but directs those books at any generation seeking a polestar for the heart on this darkening planet. Miss Boyle leaves us with Dahlberg's hymn: "So long as we communicate the truth, we move ourselves, life, history, men."

Only now is Edward Dahlberg beginning to attain the attention and understanding he deserves. If this book helps in either of these respects it will have accomplished its purpose.

HAROLD BILLINGS

The University of Texas at Austin
November 11, 1967

ACKNOWLEDGMENTS

MY DEEPEST thanks are extended to Mrs. Florence H. Williams who kindly allowed me to use William Carlos Williams' previously unpublished essay which is deposited in The University of Texas Library; to Mr. Joseph Evans Slate whose original essay in a somewhat different form was presented to the South Central Modern Language Association on October 21, 1967; and to Mr. Robert Kindrick for his essay written for this volume.

Grateful acknowledgment is expressed to the authors and publishers for permission to reprint the following essays: "An Introduction to *Bottom Dogs*" by D. H. Lawrence is reprinted from *Bottom Dogs*, published by City Lights Books, 1961; "Preface to *Bottom Dogs*" by Edward Dahlberg is reprinted from *Bottom Dogs*, published by City Lights Books, © 1961 by Edward Dahlberg; "Edward Dahlberg's Book of Lazarus" by Jonathan Williams is reprinted from *The Texas Quarterly*, Summer 1963; *"The Sorrows of Priapus"* by Sir Herbert Read is reprinted from *The Sewanee Review*, Spring 1958, copyright 1958 by The University of the South; "A Foreword to *Alms for Oblivion*" by Sir Herbert Read is reprinted from *Alms for Oblivion*, published by the University of Minnesota Press, © copyright 1964 by the University of Minnesota; "A Great Stylist: The Prophet as Critic" by Allen Tate is reprinted from *The Sewanee Review*, Spring 1961, copyright 1961 by The University of the South; "Cudgels and Distaffs, for the Rebirth . . ." by Victor Lipton is reprinted from *Prairie Schooner*, Fall 1961, copyright © 1961 by the University of Nebraska Press; "The Eloquence of Failure" by Alfred Kazin is reprinted from *The Reporter*, August 13, 1964, copyright 1964 by the Reporter Magazine Company; "Edward Dahlberg's *Because I Was Flesh*" by Josephine

9

ACKNOWLEDGMENTS

Herbst is reprinted from *The Southern Review*, Spring 1965; "*Alms for Oblivion* and Others" by Frank MacShane is reprinted from *The Southern Review*, Summer 1967; "A Man on His Own" by Frank MacShane is reprinted from *The New York Times Book Review*, March 5, 1967, © 1967 by The New York Times Company, reprinted by permission; "An Introduction to Edward Dahlberg" by Paul Carroll is reprinted from *The Edward Dahlberg Reader*, published by New Directions, copyright © 1967 by New Directions Publishing Corporation; "A Man in the Wilderness" by Kay Boyle is reprinted from *The Nation*, May 29, 1967, copyright 1967 by the Nation Associates, Inc.

In addition, I would like to thank James Laughlin, Warren Roberts, George Cogswell, Andrew Ruth, Ronald Seeliger, Joseph Cunningham, and Mrs. Mary Hirth, for various assistances.

And, finally, my gratitude to John Womack who introduced me to the writing of Edward Dahlberg.

CONTENTS

AMERICAN ISHMAEL OF LETTERS

HAROLD BILLINGS

INTRODUCTION: CABALIST IN THE WRONG SEASON

EDWARD DAHLBERG's writings are remarkable reliquaries of feeling and thought. Born in this century, he is yet out of season with our time. "We are now in the long, cold night of literature," he writes, "and most of the poems are composed in the Barren Grounds." Surely, some part of him was bred when books were better loved, when learning was a joy, when deep feeling was nourished and freely expressed. His work could be appreciated in any century in which the English language has been written.

The critical attention given Edward Dahlberg over the years has been checkered. It is unusual to find any book on the American literature of the 1930's which does not mention his autobiographical novel *Bottom Dogs*. D. H. Lawrence wrote the Introduction to that first book of Dahlberg's, perhaps unfortunately, for now any criticism of Dahlberg's work begins and ends with his statement.

Lawrence used Dahlberg's book as a basis for a fulmination against the "human stink" he found in American society; and he characterized *Bottom Dogs* and its anti-hero Lorry as mirrors of this repulsive, bottom-dog spirit—the book "a genuine book, as far as it goes, even if it is an objectionable one."

Edmund Wilson did not agree with Lawrence; in his review "Dahlberg, Dos Passos and Wilder" (*The Shores of Light*) Wilson stated, "It would be easy for a writer of another kind to make Dahlberg's kind of experience repulsive, but I do not feel that Dahlberg

15

has done so: the temperament through which he has strained his orphan homes, his barber shops and bakeries, his dance-halls and Y.M.C.A.'s, though he is always realistically observant, seems a gentle and unassertive, and, consequently, an unembittered one. We read the book, at any rate, with wonder to see how the rawest, the cheapest, the most commonplace American material may be transmuted by a man of talent, so submerged in it that he can only speak its language, yet acting upon it so strongly, so imbuing it with his own tone and color and texture, that he can make it yield a work of distinction."

Those early 1930's were restless, political years for the writer as everyone else, and Dahlberg's proletarian canticles were generally welcomed among the socialist literati as were the works of any author who touched on the tragedy of human existence. But Dahlberg has always been a wild, mustang spirit and fettered only by moral corrals, not by social or political movements. It was only natural that he should become estranged from Marxism, and a mutual bitterness still exists between him and many former fellow-travelers. Most of those writers with whom he shared pages in *New Masses*, *The New Republic*, and *The Nation* in the 1930's have been forgotten; but unfortunately for Dahlberg several hold important positions in our journals today. When he told "how venal and coarse this crew of Marxist angels was, nobody would even review a book" of his, Dahlberg has written in a letter to Allen Tate. Communism is political narcissism, economic and social self-love. As V. S. Pritchett has written, "Dahlberg is dead right about the Narcissism that ruined his contemporaries in the Twenties and Thirties. So many of them swanked themselves to death." By contrast, Dahlberg's work is stronger today than it was in 1930.

From Flushing to Calvary, a sequel to *Bottom Dogs*, was published in 1932, but gained somewhat less attention than the first book.

Then Dahlberg went to Germany, was there at the time of the Reichstag fire, and as a result wrote the anti-Nazi novel *Those Who Perish*, published in 1934. That Dahlberg remained somewhere in the fringes of left-wing acceptance for another year is evident from the reviews that *Those Who Perish* received, and from the fact that

16

Dahlberg contributed reviews of Waldo Frank and Kenneth Fearing to *New Masses* in the spring of 1935, and was an organizer of and participant in the first American Writers' Congress held the same year.

James T. Farrell reviewed *Those Who Perish* at length in *New Masses*, December 4, 1934. "In his use of imagery and symbols there is revealed a brilliant originality," Farrell said of Dahlberg; and Granville Hicks, writing of "The Novel and the Middle Class" in the same magazine on January 1, 1935, declared "most of the time [the reader] is held fast by the devastating accuracy of Dahlberg's revelation." The world has been broken, many friendships torn, and allegiances changed, in the thirty years since those reviews.

The full story of American letters in the 1930's and Dahlberg's participation has yet to be told. "I resolved as early as '34 to be a man of letters, and to be an eremite to do so," he wrote Tate in 1962. And it is apparent that Dahlberg found distaste for the stew in the State Kettle—". . . when contemporary metaphysicians and writers impugn the fetiches and taboos of the state they are prosecuted or banished," he later wrote, with possible personal overtones —and disenchantment with the tone and direction of his own writing. So he gave up his novel-in-progress "Bitch Goddess" (success), the first two chapters of which were published in *Signature* magazine, Spring 1936, and went into a period of literary apprenticeship, study, and critical limbo. For several years he seems forcibly forgotten. Only Ford Madox Ford, writing in *The Forum* in September, 1937, kept Dahlberg's name alive, naming him, William Carlos Williams, and E. E. Cummings as the three most neglected writers in America. Ford reported that Dahlberg's *Those Who Perish* had sold only two hundred copies, a figure severe as the leper's whited skin, so that no publisher would touch him. "We cannot buy enough books by one of the most brilliant pens of our day to let the holder of that pen find a publisher," Ford wrote. "It would be a scandal if Mr. Dahlberg were only a third or a fifth or a tenth less brilliant than he is." But Dahlberg went on unpublished, brewing a majestic book from his meditations that would earn him for the moment even more oblivion.

17

In 1941 Dahlberg came back to published letters still a lazar. It was with insight and the sure touch of prophecy that Dahlberg dedicated *Do These Bones Live* to his mother, "who as sorrowing Hagar, has taught me how to make Ishmael's Covenant with the Heart's Afflictions." It should be noted that Dahlberg, who has never hidden disdain or interred his thanks, made full tribute to Ford in this book. Ford was then dead, and *Do These Bones Live* joined him among the shades.

This work displayed Dahlberg with a completely new voice, radically different from the naturalistic jargon of his first books, but retaining the honesty and power that distinguishes all he writes. Dahlberg had tilled the pasturage of all literary history, and written a book on American literature that was rooted in William Carlos Williams' *In the American Grain* and D. H. Lawrence's *Studies in Classic American Literature*. *Do These Bones Live* is an indictment of Puritanism and Statism, Naturalism and Rationalism, and was reviewed rather warmly by Alfred Kazin in the *Herald-Tribune*, who commented "there is a fragment of greatness here"; but the *American Mercury*, invoking the name of a writer dear to Dahlberg, buried him with Chaucer's "No more of this, for Godde's dignitee." And in 1942 in his *On Native Grounds*, Kazin wrote of Dahlberg's early proletarian novels, but asserted he was "exhausted by his own sensibility."

Do These Bones Live sold fewer than 375 copies, Dahlberg relates; and *The Flea of Sodom*, that small, rich book of fable which followed in 1950, had few reviews and sold feebly when first published.

The daybreak of critical appreciation of the work of Dahlberg's maturity began, not with a review but with a preface—that by Herbert Read to the London edition of *Do These Bones Live*, published in 1947 under the title *Sing O Barren*. In that preface Read spoke of the "rich expressive beauty" of Dahlberg's style, and his "all-pervasive human wisdom." Read also introduced *The Flea of Sodom*, "a book like Nietzsche's, for all and none; a book, also, for all time." And Read indirectly challenged *Ulysses* and *Finnegans Wake* to stand beside Dahlberg's book.

Even *The New Yorker* called the publication of *The Flea of*

Sodom "a rare event," the book filled with "a fury and eloquence lost to us since the death of D. H. Lawrence." But the book, and Dahlberg, were soon lost.

It was seven years before Dahlberg was published again: *The Sorrows of Priapus* (1957), only half the text being chiseled from Dahlberg's manuscript, the remainder to be published in 1968 under the title *The Carnal Myth*. Professor Joseph Slate, in a display of neglected books at The University of Texas in 1961, described *The Sorrows* as "perhaps the most original book of American prose since *Walden*, a dense but imaginative combination of myth and social commentary." Significantly, Dr. Slate was one of the first scholars to salute Dahlberg. In *American Quarterly*, Winter 1958, Slate said of *The Sorrows*: "Unclassifiable, a cataloguer's nightmare, this book touches so many kinds of American studies—history, literary criticism, sociology and geography—that one is tempted to call it unique."

On the other hand, the poet Robert Duncan viciously attacked the book in *Poetry* as an example of "the sympathetic heart broken," Dahlberg almost a literary antichrist—an attack based, it seems to me, on a completely fallacious reading of the book.

Truth Is More Sacred (1961) had much the same mixed critical reception; but *Because I Was Flesh* (1964) may have achieved whatever apotheosis Dahlberg is to have. Not enough can be said for this great book, perhaps the finest prose work composed by a twentieth-century American. The statements lauding it by many of the finest writers are singularly admiring. The book was runner-up for the National Book Award of 1964; and one can wonder, dispassionately, at the politics of such awards.

Dahlberg's books published since that date have had their usual varied reviews. A man so passionately at odds with the modern world, a man so dedicated to the truth as he sees it, so opposed to current literary orthodoxy, is bound to engender a mutually passionate response, outcries of either rage or admiration.

Any independent, uncompromising writer runs the risk of wrong readers, misunderstanding, neglect. His writing is more likely to have lovers than critics. He writes to please himself, not the moment. Dahlberg strides through American literature as independ-

19

ently as Thoreau through Concord, and can say with him, "I long ago lost a hound, a bay horse, and a turtledove, and am still on their trail."

All those critics who cleave deeply into the quick of Dahlberg's style remark its passionate roots in the great humanistic masters of prose. And Dahlberg would affirm that in those masters lies the virtue of his own writing. "A good writer is a gifted reader," Dahlberg says. "When writing flags it means that people are forgetting how to study, and no longer go to Seneca or to Cicero or to Blake to fortify their character." Dahlberg feeds on the classics. Consider the bizarre catalogue of writers and works he instructs the poet and translator Anthony Kerrigan to read on the road to the mountains of letters: "Macrobius, Pausanias, Herodian, Suetonius, Clement of Alexandria, Josephus, the *Moralia* of Plutarch, the Elizabethans, the writers of the Comedy of the Restoration, Livy, Thucydides, Coleridge's *Biographia Literaria*, Dryden's *Essays*, Ruskin's *Praeterita*, Herzen, Saint-Simon, Pliny, Strabo, Dionysius of Halicarnassus, and sundry other authors and savants."

It is hardly enough to say that Dahlberg's prose is like any one or all of the writers he admires. He uses all in a unique way. For he absorbs style, the style he finds true to him, into the very marrow of his literary bones. He does not mimic; he makes what he finds good in another writer into a parcel of his own writing nature. In *Can These Bones Live* (as this book was re-titled in its 1960 edition) Dahlberg discusses the Greek artist who masqueraded beneath "the skin of a beast or the feathers of a bird" (and here he is quoting from Jane Harrison's *Ancient Art and Ritual*) so as to "emphasize, enlarge, enhance his own personality." There is no other way to enlarge one's self and, as Dahlberg says, "express the world." It is the resonance of Dahlberg's style and thought through the influence of the great masters that moves him toward myth. Subject and style demand one another. *Only* fable can enlarge life to so express the world.

Karl Shapiro recently, and rather sarcastically, commented: "Dahlberg's thoughts and sayings are always clothed in Palladian or Tudor millinery (when he is not reciting Ecclesiastes). One is never sure how seriously to take him . . . To thunder in full dress is only temporarily effective; when the lights go up one is embarrassed." The state of our letters today is evidently so dishonest that the forthright stance of Dahlberg is suspect. The simple is hardest to believe: that Dahlberg is precisely what, and how, he says. For style and man are one. The skin and feathers of his mythologic masquerade have, so to speak, grafted to the twentieth-century man. Shapiro must realize this, for he admits Dahlberg's "blind loyalty to himself as poet, prophet, and *l'inconnu*—these are his birthright, by all means. No one in his right mind could envy him, except a poet."

Dahlberg's values hew to those ancient Hebraic laws that prescribe justice, familial honor, and humility. In all his writing can be seen the pendulum swing of the head and the heart of the Judaic prophets: the earth was created for man but man must again become part of that earth. Man sings high, but must go low. He erects his manhood, then grovels in the dirt. This is a paradox of life; who was less vain than Job on his muckheap questioning the Lord's might?

I suspect there are enough contradictions in the fearful symmetry of Edward Dahlberg to allow him to escape critical sanctification. Granitic, living works defy definition, distillation, evaporation, the alchemical processes of the critic. But certain recurrent themes may be sieved from Dahlberg's works. The forms, the words, the backdrops change, but these themes are as constant to Dahlberg as the stars in their watches.

Wholeness, of man, of art, of life, is possibly the chief theme that permeates Dahlberg's writing. It is desire for wholeness that has made him despair at the American's loss of his past and parent, his sodomous fusion of cultures, the European lamb burned on a savage American altar. (Is anti-Semitism the violent and vicious rejection of a religious parent? Is much avant-garde writing the childish casting away of literary heritage?) Dahlberg likes to paraphrase William Carlos Williams saying the conquerors of America were overcome by the wild, vast weight of the continent. The resultant illness of our social corpus is reflected in individual homosexuality, unrest, frustration, and rationalism.

The non-rational, contradictory "reasons of the heart"—man's

21

fatuous carnality and tragic spirituality—the doubled pulse of life and death—self-love and self-loathing: all go into Dahlberg's conception of human wholeness. The mathematic man lies in Ezekiel's Valley; the man of feeling is the Dahlbergian ideal, shaken into "prophetic commotion" by his sensibilities.

Dahlberg's views on America's lost and buried birthright—a cultural and spiritual Eden, if you will—appear and reappear in the compulsive symbolism of Cain and Abel, as Allen Tate has written of in his Preface to Dahlberg's poems, *Cipango's Hinder Door*. Abel is our historical heritage, our innocence and feeling, the nonrational pulse, slain by Cain and buried in the soil. Dahlberg, unlike the American who pours gasoline on the herbs in his heart, prays for a return to woods, fields, and stone-fences in the spirit.

Perversity Dahlberg sees as flux, the muck-tides of our cities, instability, the shriek of catamites and the pad of the Machine through cement and asphalt forests. Movement is the sensual water sin. "Everything we do is for going somewhere else, and a people who have no strength to sit still and think are ready for any sort of change, upheaval or debacle," he writes. "They cannot be quiet enough to read or love a wife."

Dahlberg's literary criticism is replete with extensions of his symbolic search for wholeness; his constant effort is to free our great writers from obdurate accretions that weaken them. This is what D. H. Lawrence had in mind when he once described the Bible as "a book that has been temporarily killed for us, or for some of us, by having its meaning arbitrarily fixed." Dahlberg's iconoclasm is not always properly understood. Robert Duncan, for instance, declared, "Like Thersites, Dahlberg maligns without principle"; a ridiculous statement. Paracelsus cast Avicenna into the fire; Dahlberg dipped Melville in nitre. And he excoriates himself no less than any other. "We cannot perceive what we canonize," he writes in *Can These Bones Live*. "O, let man laugh the *gods* out of this world so that the heart can live in it!"

Puritanism, another inversion, has long drawn his wrath. *Can These Bones Live* is, in part, in the simplest definition, an indictment of Puritanism with the marvelous and supernatural murder of American literature. "Purge the flesh and you canker the spirit."

Touchless, crutched humans were whitewashed; their austere furniture tells us of their dour feelings. Sex became flagellation, walking a phallic plank, bundling with a board, and the search for privy teats. The American still has Puritanism templed and pewed in his soul. "Afraid of touching anybody lest he be infected by a germ, he is unable to catch the most important of all human diseases, affection," Dahlberg writes of the American pleb. And our literature is similarly withered: "Almost the whole of American literature has been a deep refusal of man . . . a renunciation of the carnal heart." Edward Dahlberg celebrates all that is human, particularly Woman: "God bless Sarah, Hagar, Rebecca, Rachel, and Bilhah, Jacob's concubine whom Reuben trod; for sufficient unto the day are the nipples and the womb thereof."

In his timeless wedding of fact and fable, Dahlberg elevates momentary experience to universal event. Thus, enlarge his life and translate the Helmet of Mambrino. His identification with Job and Ishmael in his work is evident to most readers; and there are other anagogic roles he assumes in his writing, in a cycle of Sinai and the Wilderness, in guilt and expiation, as Adam, Cain, Abel, Lazarus, as Jesus, Barabbas, and Judas. Dahlberg goes to biblical mythology, that Cave of Machpelah, as though it were the Globe Theatre's visionary cloakroom. By invoking legendary names in the mythification of his own experience there are creative feelings generated within us that draw sustenance and meaning from these characters. Awareness of his use of such symbols can enrich the reading eye, if we do not become lost in a perverse, theoretical search for their spoor.

Man's separation from man, exaggerated for Dahlberg by his orphaned years, is a poignant theme in his art. He voices a universal lament at the lorn wastes of man's spirit. The sixth chapter of *Because I Was Flesh* could have been ripped from some ancient holy text on solitude, but this is the American West of the 1910's:

How or when I came to Needles, California, I do not know. What had I gained from my misfortunes? I crept into coal cars, and snow, hail and rain were my roof. When I had to flee from a brakeman with a club or from a plain-clothes man, I would slink into a town of asphalt taken from the Dead Sea. Trudging over countless guts of cement that ran like slag in Gehenna, I stuffed my scabrous shoes with newspapers. My suit was a sickness; the moth sighed in my shirt and trousers. I was threadbare, hungered when I ate and imprisoned when I was free. I swallowed sleet, wind and confusion. Was I wandering on a peopleless comet without herbs, grass or ocean? How much punishment can the body take without corrupting the spirit? Could I feed upon my sores and not stink? My hair fell out in large clumps, and when I viewed the miserable remnants of my boyhood, vultures appeared. I moaned for my youth, for I was only nineteen at the time; baldness had come upon Gaza and my bones sang in the cinders and waste places of Jerusalem.

It is remarkable that a poet can wring such words from the feeling but unspeaking heart. Nietzsche spoke of the vision generated by a dance. The reader of Dahlberg's tragedy is a participant in its visionary suffering and triumph. Man would long ago have been buried by his own feelings had he no prophet, priest, or poet to free him. Ritual, prayer, and poetry save us from ourselves. The poet assumes a cross under which any man might tremble. Dahlberg realizes this when he calls Shakespeare the Christ of literature. And Dahlberg bears the burden of his own amazing voice. His sorrow is a song for the reader who cannot sing.

Readers of *Because I Was Flesh* know the influence exerted on Edward Dahlberg by his mother Lizzie, the only touchstone that endured his youth and orphaned heart. If there is one element that transforms the bleak barber basin of *Bottom Dogs* into the golden helmet of *Because I Was Flesh* it is the death of Dahlberg's mother. For in her death, his great loss, he found some reconciliation with life itself.

"It would be idle to say that Lizzie Dahlberg, whose bones still have sentience, is what she was. She is and she is not, and that is the difference between the trance we call being and the other immense experience we name death . . . She only questioned God in anger once: 'Why am I miserable, while others who are pitiless and contemptible are so fortunate?' But she never received an answer.

Not God, but gibing Pilate came to her and asked, 'What is Truth?'
And I knew not why until I had heard her quiet reply: 'My life.' "

Dahlberg's personal grief begets vision. At one time or another,
he has confessed to cynicism, nihilism, pessimism—but through his
own tormented humanity Dahlberg's negations approach prophetic
affirmation. The striving of Sisyphus is his faith; and he has made
his own myth from the South American guanaco: "No ancient bar-
row or cenotaph is more noble than the dying guanaco, who crawls
to the marge of a river to leave his bones by the waters. His end is
more important than his life. We would be indifferent to human
fate were it not that man dies."

Edward Dahlberg has written the apocryphal books of American
literature: psalms, admonitions, exhortations, proverbs, riddles,
prohibitions, contrasts, beatitudes, similes, wise counsel, and woes.
We are all Lots in this modern Sodom and how should we live
bereft of literary angels?

Dahlberg closes his Introduction to *Epitaphs of Our Times*, that
epistolary collection of "madness, follies, dissimulation, turbulent
and incoherent thoughts and peevish and dour moods," with these
lines addressed to Edwin Seaver: "A cabalist, born in the wrong
season, I beseech you, live long, which has eight letters, twice those
contained in spelling love." Cabalist, yes; and love above all.

What then, finally, is Dahlberg's person, and what is his work?

There is a dream of Jesus in *Because I Was Flesh*. And how
much more of the book is real, and how much dream, makes little
difference. The historical reality of Edward Dahlberg is no more
important than that of Christ. For as Dahlberg says, ". . . the only
real history is the mythical one. Soon as a man dies he is a legend.
Man must eat fables, or starve his soul to death."

Modern American literature, full as it is of rationalism and
naturalism, is poor soil for fable. Cabalist in the wrong season, a
prophet still without honor, it is Edward Dahlberg's distinction that
he has grown parables in this earth. His works are myth, and they
are splendid.

25

JONATHAN WILLIAMS

EDWARD DAHLBERG'S BOOK OF LAZARUS

And I said, "O defiled flock, take a harp, and chant to the ancient relics, lest understanding perish." Then I labored for the miracle of seeing and knowing, and thought I heard murmuring Euphrates, and perceived the first-born leaves of Eden whose savor of apple, elm and hazel-nut garnished the lips of Jehovah. But it was nothing, and my spirit was a mute tomb.

THE PRECEDING inscription is the most concise statement of Edward Dahlberg's position I can find. It occurs in that sedulously ignored little volume, *The Flea of Sodom*. It is because of such ignoring that I undertake the explication of my own reading of his work. God knows, I do not have the prodigious knowledge of classic literatures clearly necessary. Nor the cast of mind of a Talmudist. Edward Dahlberg in his sixty-third year can say, with Robert Burton: ". . . confined to the company of the distinguished, I have spent thirty-seven full and fortunate years. . . ." Which is a lot of reading and experience. Yet, the work insists. I only hope it will lead others to a thorough job. But let this be said at the outset about Dahlberg, and I again quote Burton, in *The Anatomy of Melancholy*, who is himself quoting Agrippa. "He speaks stones and let his readers beware lest he break their heads."

27

I: Three "Scatological Mistakes"

By 1928 Dahlberg had written his first novel, *Bottom Dogs*. D. H. Lawrence, who earlier had written a long preface to Maurice Magnus' *Memoirs of the Foreign Legion*, contributed an introduction. Arabella York, second wife of Richard Aldington and one of the heroines in *Aaron's Rod*, sent Lawrence the manuscript. He seems to have found both these books specimens of an extremist nature which fascinated as a serpent might. (Dahlberg in allowing a reprint of *Bottom Dogs* in 1961 insisted on the right to attack his own novel and Lawrence's notion of it in a new prefatory note.) And it is true that much of Lawrence's case for and against *Bottom Dogs* now seems unproven.

The book is a series of vignettes. It begins in Kansas City in the Teddy Roosevelt era and concerns Lizzie Lewis, a lady barber, and her young son Lorry. Lizzie had run off from her husband, a fur operator in Brooklyn, with a barber years ago. He turned out to be a chippie-chaser and a pimp, so she ducked him in Dallas, Denver, Memphis, etc., and landed in K.C. Lizzie takes up with a river man, "Kentucky Blue Grass Henry Smith," who wants Lorry out of the way. Lorry is dispatched to an orphanage in Cleveland. The three chapters which follow seem to be the ones that astonished Lawrence: "There I realized with amazement how rapidly the human psyche can strip itself of its awareness and its emotional contacts, and reduce itself to a subbrutal condition of simple gross persistence. It is not animality—far from it. These boys are much less than animals. They are cold wills functioning with a minimum of consciousness. The amount that they are *not* aware of is perhaps the most amazing aspect of their character. They are brutally and deliberately unaware. They have no hopes, no desires even. They have even no will-to-exist, for existence even is too high a term. They have a strange, stony will-to-persist, that is all. And they persist by reaction, because they still feel the repulsiveness of each other, of everything, even of themselves. . . . It is, in psychic disintegration, a good many stages ahead of *Point Counter Point*." Which just isn't so. As a matter of fact *Bottom Dogs* strikes me as much closer to *Huckleberry Finn* than to *The Blackboard Jungle* or

Rebel Without a Cause. The cool generation would have given Lawrence a real *crise de fois.* For instance, and here is Dahlberg writing:

> Sometimes then they would wander around, get a sack of cherries from a huckster, and shoot the pits at alley-cats. On their way back they would blow themselves to a pint of ice cream, scoop it out with pieces of pasteboard from the box, and sing on the front porch in their b.v.d.s: 'The bells are ringing for me and my gal.' That would get Max into a chatty vein and he would ramble along like a 1916 Ford. Was Werner, the gardener, really the kaiser's bodyguard, and how many more weeks would Werner's nag last? Max said he had once tried to ride him, but that the old dobbin was harder than Doc's nails, and that he almost split in two.

That is hardly psychopathic or reptilian. It is, to admit it, about the maximum warmth evidenced anywhere in the book, but this is not *Penrod* or *Peck's Bad Boy.* (Dahlberg's quarrel with his book is in its use of vernacular: "I once wrote to Sherwood Anderson and told him that *Winesburg, Ohio* was right and that *Bottom Dogs* was wrong because his was warm and human and mine was written in a rough, bleak idiom.") Yet it is, of course, the veracity of the book that continues to impress us. The portraits of two orphans, Herman Mush Tate and Bonehead-Star-Wolfe, are memorably drawn, as well as the minor appearances of Prunes, Shrimp, and Doc. From the orphanage the story moves back to Kansas City and then Lorry decides to go on the bum—to Salt Lake City, Portland, Frisco, and into L.A., where he takes up residence at the Y.M.C.A. Again, there is a lot of acuity in this writing. It is sharp and mordant; he is writing about a sleazy down-and-out world and doing it with gusto. "The After Bible Coffee Class" is a wild scene. *Bottom Dogs* ends in Solomon's Dancepalace. Lorry sees an hallucinatory vision of the City—"God, he hadn't really known he had been up against all that. . . . Perhaps, he would go east, get out of it all, he could run away; but he couldn't go side-door Pullman again, that was finished. Boing, sleeping in coal cars, riding those railroad bronchos, going to strange hotel rooms, the ghastly plaster inside those empty clothesclosets, walking the streets—all that was done, but then, how did he know? Anyhow, if he got the clap he would go to the Los Angeles City Hospital; maybe, those enamelled iron beds, the sheets, the medical immaculateness of it all, might do something to him. Something had to happen; and he knew nothing would. . . ."

From Flushing to Calvary continues the story of Lizzie and Lorry and is set in Bensonhurst, Queens—"Cheap peoples live here." Lizzie has given up barbering and supplements Lorry's random income by paring neighbors' corns, giving violet-ray treatments, and supplying an old Indian remedy as a quack abortionist. I quote several of the author's remarks about the book that appeared in *Contempo*, October 25, 1932, Chapel Hill, N.C.:

> There is a long procession of other characters in the book. Lizzie's marital prospects, pregnant patients, their chronicle of opinions and schemes: and they are just as anxious to do her as she them. . . . It is no longer the scene so much, as in *Bottom Dogs*, which is the protagonist, as the kick-about figures who pass through it, for they never act but react upon their environment. . . . Both Lizzie and Lorry have a nostalgia for the past, which is as horrific and harrowing as the present, but which appears less so, because it is the past, and because at least they have their roots there. She still regrets the day that she gave up her lady-barber shop, and Lorry wants to and does run away from his mother to return to the orphanage in Cleveland. And only then does he discover that he is in no place and that no place is in him. . . . The inevitability of failure of the dollarless American trapped in a capitalistic society is one of the essential themes of the book. . . . What the author has tried to indicate here is not Lawrence's *Look! We Have Come Through*, but Look! What has come through us! . . . I understand that one of the small, insurgent magazines has listed *Bottom Dogs* among the 'defeatist' novels. Now for one thing, this seems to me to be a piece of egregiously sick leftism. Of course, it is true that all the bottom dog drifters and Y.M.C.A. white collarites are ineluctably doomed at the outset of the novel. But no matter what one may charge this gelatinous mass of floating population with, it is certainly inac-

curate to lay defeatism upon their backs also, because that implies a choice, which they have never had, simply because they never knew they had one. For one of the very few reasons that they don't take their hunger and social abasement singing the *Internationale* is that they have never heard of it. Never heard of Communism. Words like *Bolshevism* either do not exist in their vocabulary at all, or are at best a kind of obscenity to be included in the national lavatory esoterica. . . . In the final chapter of *From Flushing to Calvary* there is Lorry, starving and derelict, caught up in a Communist riot at Union Square. An innocent bystander, he has been the victim of one of Grover Whalen's courteous cops. Lying on the pavement, the blood stingingly humming over the wound, he furtively lifts his head. A red flag is floppily streaming around the corner. It looks to him like one of those auctioneer's flags he has seen in front of furniture warehouses. . . . Through Washington Square and out of the book he walks, tightening his belt, the blood clotting over his head, and chanting a chapel hymn which he had sung when he was an inmate of an orphan asylum in Cleveland: *neath its folds, defeat unknown / triumph, crowns our glorious way.* . . . Now in order to please the Communists I might have had Lorry at the end dash up to the *New Masses* offices or elsewhere and ask for membership in the Party. But then I would no longer be a novelist but a liar. For this would no more be possible for Lorry than for that other pathetic American protagonist in Dreiser's *An American Tragedy*.

Yet, again despite the inexorable forces and intentions of the book's message, Lizzie's vitality pours through it and her death in the hospital is heartrending. There is no keeping her down and Lorry is not stopped for long either: "If he had a little extra change, he took a street-car ride out to the end of the Santa Monica, as he sang out loud to himself:

> i'm a lord of paradox.
> i'm an autocrat of passion.

Then he leaned out of the window of the jersey-red Santa Monica streetcar, the California bungalows and the billposter lawns flowing past him in hightide, and recited to himself:

'in the beginning was the word,' metempsychosis, metamorphosis, transmigration, protagoras, transcendentalism, swedenborgianism, swedenborgian fungi . . .

And with a singing elocutional belief, he continued, sinking himself into it:

> *o rhodora*
> *if the sages ask thee why*
> *this charm is wasted on earth and sky*
> *tell them dear . . .*

The roofs of the bungalows formed gabled spouting waves. They billowed and tossed, and as they came in they seemed to wash up against the street-car windows as surf. He went right along with it:

de profundis, out of the depths, dorian dorian the portrait of dorian gray, theophile gautier, multifarious, asphodel, santa monica, capistrano, monterey, carmel-by-the-sea . . .

> *by the sea*
> *by the sea*
> *by the beautiful sea*
> *i left my ship in avalon . . .*

Lorry was singing right out, his voice perforating the *Los Angeles Examiner* behind him. He couldn't hold himself back:

bhagavad-gita . . . bhagavad-gita . . . bhagavad-gita . . . the oversoul . . .

> *true brahmin, in the morning meadows wet,*
> *exposed the vedas and the violet.*

Then he kept on repeating some newfound words he had just picked up from a book he had bought at Parker's bookshop on 6th:

hyperbole, hyperbole, anthropomorphic, hyacinthine, arroyo secco . . .

32

The *Los Angeles Examiner* behind him crackled and was creased into hard knuckle points and whisked into a pocket. The *Examiner*, bobbing up and down very perkily in the coatpocket like a smart-aleck punch-and-judy, leaned out and bent down, as the man took another seat with a— 'You goddam looney idiot.' Lorry craned his neck around toward it as it sprang back in the pocket. Then something went dead in him, and he got off at the next stop and caught another streetcar."

The passage makes me note a quotation by Lenny Bruce: "All my humor is based upon destruction and despair. If the whole world were tranquil, without disease and violence, I'd be standing in the breadline—right back of J. Edgar Hoover."

The third of the early novels, *Those Who Perish*, was the first American fiction to concern itself with Nazism in the United States. Dahlberg had been in Germany prior to and during Hitler's assumption of power and was a member of the executive board of the National Committee for the Defense of Political Prisoners. *Those Who Perish* are a group of Jews—directors and workers connected with the Community House in a New Jersey city called New Republic. The three principal figures are Regina Gordon, Joshua Boaz, and Eli Melamed. Each finally dies of a bewildering network of persecutions and petty daily horrors. The following passage gives the book's exact flavor:

Regina Gordon was still lying back on the couch, propped up against cretonne and velvet cushions, and staring at the Chippendale pieces banked in thick migraine clouds which scudded past her. She had one of those full, hemicranial attacks which are one of the closest approximations to boredom, and which had the same oppressive effect upon her as a long tedious voyage on a rodent bulbous sea, the only memories of which are the paint, the engine oil, and the ship's disinfectant that invariably seem to permeate tourist and third-class lavatories. The living-room was cluttered with objects of art: a gold-plated Swiss clock, a synagogical brass candelabra, an imitation Javanese print, a litter of brass and majolica animals. The planetarium touch which appeared to pervade the apartment was supplied by two man-sized cactuses set in copper urns. Besides these, there was an odd assortment of

33

goldfish. Any one making his initial visit to her apartment might have thought that Regina Gordon was in hiding, as it were, and that she was subconsciously attempting to fill up the gaps of her existence so that it would not be so devastatingly simple. As for the effect she had upon the more cultivated middle-class mothers of the children with whom she worked and who occasionally came to see her, Regina's voice, rising and falling amid the stale majolica animals in the room, cast the same spell upon them that the simple bell-like exercises issuing from a studio on Michigan Boulevard might have upon a young man from Omaha or Davenport. For them Regina Gordon belonged to that class of charming women who do their shopping in the antique places on Madison and Lexington avenues, who have psychoanalysts as friends, but who are still conformists enough to say, 'But must we have Communism?' For herself, she did not know to whom or what she belonged. Had she lived in a less tragic age, her conversational vocabulary would have included more such names and words as Gautier, George Moore, Richard Burton, Anatole France, onyx, sapphire, Oscar Wilde, and less of Bolshevism, Marx, Lenin, and Fascism. As it was, the one vocabulary canceled the other, and the two rarely, if ever, co-existed in her consciousness. At one time she was a devotee of classical regularity: order, a home, a large garden-bed, pewter from Bruges, pottery from Limoges, rare first editions. Now all these things were burdens, and whenever she arranged a few flowers in a vase or held Sweet Williams in her hand, she felt all the sadness of acting or viewing something out of the context of one's times. All that belonged to another period, before the World War and the Russian Revolution, before the Nazi Terror, and it could never come back. She could not even wish for it, and no sooner did she think of it than it stuck in her throat. And yet . . . and yet . . . she thought of a tall glass of tea she had once had in Quebec during a vacation. It was flavored with mint leaves and recalled the wild vacant lots over-run with knee-deep razor-edged grass and sunflowers, which she had played in as a child. Before the Nazi Terror, New Republic, the Community House, Joshua, his yearnings for a communal life in a lemon grove outside of Tel Aviv . . . she could still see him sitting in the puce-upholstered armchair, his hair nervously kinking in front . . . Puce, puce . . . Regina twisted the word puce like a fresh bedewed stalk between her fingers. . . .

At the end Regina takes poison: "As she sank to the floor, her mouth parted in drunken jubilation, she swept her arms out. 'For those who have the heart for tomorrow,' and then she smouldered into yesterday." When I first read *Those Who Perish* some four or five years ago I did not find it comparable with its two predecessors. (To clarify a possible confusion: *Kentucky Blue Grass Henry Smith*, though published separately in a limited edition, is, in fact, the final section of *From Flushing to Calvary*.) Now I find otherwise. This is really the first work in which he probes the motivations of his characters. The Hitlerian spectre, the enormities of the depression forced Dahlberg into that familiar dilemma of the thirties. In 1935, for instance, one finds him writing an introduction for Kenneth Fearing's *Poems* and saying: "And as the poems in their chronological progression become more incisive and attain Marxian lucidity the ironic comments rise and expand into an affirmative Communist statement." Whatever the truth or error of that statement *Those Who Perish* is a humane, affecting document. Another virtue is that the prose almost never suffers instances of: "She held the olive, a melancholy Da Vinci green, between her fingers. As Boaz gazed at the olive and then at her hair, which then looked like rain-fresh blueberries in a market basket, he was saddened by her pessimism." There are a series of images of the physiognomy in the first two novels that can only be termed horrendous; e.g.: "Lucy unleashed her knee, her turquoise seagreen dress rivering above it, her teeth softly limelighting her pursed-up lips." . . . "Her oyster-shell gray eyes gave off a penny-machine-slot glint." . . . "She called him, her teeth, stupid wide-apart kernels of bantam corn." . . . "her throat, which had become as loose and sagging as an empty untied bull-durham sack . . ." . . . "The tears running down her neck seemed to leak out of her throat which looked like a crinkled up broken paperbag." . . . "The hair he had looked like a scrubby, low, jagged backyard fence running around the edge of his pot-shaped head." . . . "Her deep breathing was the aggravated puffing hiss of a boiling-over automobile radiator." . . . "Her eyes were moving-picture epitaphs in her head." . . . "He stared at her 14-karat solid-gold tooth tap-dancing before the semicircular footlights of her false whiteteeth." Help. Thirty years later Dahlberg laments his youthful subservience to the "abominable tongue." "Plain humble words have more health in them than the latest neologism invented by an advertising scribbler whose sole aim is to sell an adulterated product to a foolish populace. Edmond Goncourt spoke of the craze of originality that had been the curse of literature in his own day. A great deal of the fugitive, humbug vocabulary is what D. H. Lawrence called the American fetish of the wild and repulsive."

II. The Testament

And he will be a wild man; his hand will be against every man, and every man's hand against him; and he shall dwell in the presence of all his brethren.

Genesis, 16:12

Edward Dahlberg calls himself Ishmael and dedicates his next book, *Do These Bones Live*, "to the memory of my Mother, Elizabeth Dahlberg, who, as sorrowing Hagar, taught me how to make Ishmael's Covenant with the Heart's Afflictions." As Ishmael, then, he is a wild man, a loner. This is the Dahlbergian secret since the beginning and I do not think I wrong him by quoting Robert Burton on solitude: "*solitude* prompts us to all kinds of evil; this solitude undoeth us, 'tis a destructive solitariness. These men are Devils alone, as the saying is, a man alone is either a Saint or a Devil; his mind is either dull or devilish; and, in this sense, woe be to him that is so alone! These wretches do frequently degenerate from men, and of sociable creatures become beasts, monsters, inhuman, ugly to behold, *misanthropes,* they do even loathe themselves, and hate the company of men . . ." It *is* man-killing to look at one's doom and say simply: "A poem or a book that does not make the reader toil for his fate deprives him of energy, which is his most tragical and valiant weapon against the cosmos, and without which man is neither epic nor universal. A book that weakens human will is inartistic, for all writing is heroic feigning, imagining that though everything perish, a book will be perdurable. Knowing that death is always brushing our backs, we write to forget death." (From "A Long Lotus Sleep," *Poetry*, February, 1953.) By this fierce standard Dahlberg judged his novels symptomatic of the disorders and in no ways curative. "Remembrance is a torn, placeless ghost, raw and wandering, unless we bury our griefs and pains in one specific ground, region, and sod. Ghosts, too, must be seeded like fruit, rains, and despair, if they are not to return to make of our hearts their Acheron, for hell is going to and fro in the earth, and having no landmarks, or country, or epitaph to define our souls." Thus it is that Dahlberg ceased writing the "proletarian" novels of his youth. A fourth of these, *Bitch Goddess,* apparently he abandoned in course. Only two chapters were printed, in *Signature* magazine, Spring 1936. Had this been the end of his career we would probably remember Edward Dahlberg in the same bemused breath with Robert McAlmon, John Hermann, James T. Farrell, Mike Gold, Maxwell Bodenheim, Erskine Caldwell, Holger Cahill, Henry Roth, Samuel Ornitz, and a handful of others.

But in 1941 the new Dahlberg book appeared. *Do These Bones Live* is, simply, a ranging attack on the Modern World, on you, on me, on every disintegration and blight of American civilization, on the superstitions of Totalitarian Man—his machined logic and the sterility of an armature with no flesh. This testament is delivered with a prose authority of the most formidable density, and consequently is not a "simple" book. It demands time to live with, respect, and humility. The author excoriates himself in the process. Elsewhere (in a section of the current autobiography-in-progress "Because I Was Flesh") he writes: "Let me now say that I have not the least respect for my moral nature. I do what I am, and though I would do otherwise, I cannot. I do not say this easily, but with infernal pain in my heart. Perhaps after many years in libraries, I can prattle better than I did. Had not Addison or Steele asserted that no one was any better for beholding a Venus done by Praxiteles?"

37

Beyond this, *Do These Bones Live* cultivates the entire heritage of western literature and morale. One imagines that Dahlberg operated the factory where David bought his slingshots. He even quarried the stones. For Plato is quoted as saying over and over that knowledge is reminiscence. One of the chief arguments is that in America the refusal of memory has given us a religion of place and a subsequently enfeebled batch of writers crawling with localist nostalgia and adolescence. "American civilization is 'deanimated,' 'metronomic,' a grotesque enlargement of that 'gap between touch and thing,' as William Carlos Williams writes in *Jacataqua*."

The title essay is a series of examinations of our chief writers: Melville, Poe, Whitman, Thoreau, Emily Dickinson, Sherwood Anderson. The native, aboriginal intelligence is not treated piously —Whitman just barely proving more cosmically useful than Mary Baker Eddy's hygiene course. "The fetish of originality is our curse. Dante took a guide!" Puritanism is considered in all its deadly detail. "Purge the flesh and you canker the spirit." Dahlberg remembers Thoreau's episode at Walden Pond of wanting to eat a muskrat to stifle his flesh-repulsion. And we have the legend of Miss Dickinson's starving in her father's garden, though Jay Leyda's new book may have news for us. Dahlberg writes: "In almost a hundred years of American Literature we do not have one feeding, breeding, sexual male, not one suffering, bed-pining Manon Lescaut or a Shulamite. There are no ripe women here . . . We have spectral essences, odorless and hueless . . . When you deny the male and female, as they are, eating, sexually throbbing and giving off dense physical emanations, then you have the great STINK. Our misanthropy comes from one thing only, not man's poverty, politics, government, but from the revulsion from his own ordure." (It is true that if one is really hip to Modern America he can learn to stop at only those motels whose johns are antiseptically 'presealed.')

Yet, I wonder if this indictment, as the author suggests elsewhere on another subject, is not casting out the devils and entering the swine? It is a dangerous doctrine if one is going to take writing as canonical scripture. The charge is: sexual confusion—starvation, disembodiedness, sodomy. "To damn sensuality, laughter and irony, Cotton Mather had turned woman into a witch: Poe took the infernal witch, begot by Mather, and buried her alive; Melville exorcised her! Lady Dickinson hid in Christ's bosom." If this is to be the measure of a writing man (and literary style *is* the man), then one has to ask questions: should poor Melville have been allowed to work in that customs house for those ruinous decades? He would have been a security risk to the State if he really thought *those* thoughts about pale Nathaniel Hawthorne. Certainly, Walt Whitman should not be allowed to ride streetcars or visit army hospitals!

I make this purposely mocking and ridiculous because the human animal (which, as Mr. Dahlberg says of himself, does what it is) has *every* right to defend its privacy. Maybe I misread the intention of this attack, for in another section of the book we find: "To deny evil is to deprive the bones of penance and to shed forever the cry of Abel's blood, the existence of Saul, Sodom, and sin of Lot's daughters, Judas Iscariot. However man may come to Being and Deity, the poor, panting Word, or absolute suffering atheism—to refuse What Is in man, his most perfidious whoring tumults, is to steal his grace." Exactly—and that I, for one, accept, though, perhaps not every definition of what is Good and Evil. "Good and Evil are inseparable; beast and man are sewn together with threads of heaven."

The chapter on Randolph Bourne, "In the Saddle of Rozinante," is a wonderful, restorative act. How few writers and readers there are who know anything of Randolph Bourne. One of the first things a devoted reader of *Do These Bones Live* will do is procure a copy of *The History of a Literary Radical & Other Papers* (which, I hope, is still in print, having been republished by *S. A. Russell*, New York, 1956). Dahlberg is right to point out that Bourne's attack on the State is the strongest in our literature since Thoreau's essays on civil disobedience. This chapter is joined by others exposing the visions of Dostoevski, Shakespeare, Christ, and Cervantes. Edward Dahlberg always begins and ends as a quixotist: "Man pursues a desperate philosophy of gallant idealism and lives and hopes and cankers with a defiant flourish. With inextinguishable fervor he ceaselessly creates his cycle of sonnets, music, art, ethics, and then with a chivalric irony wraps the worms in the Golden Fleece of Colchis."

Sir Herbert Read says of *The Flea of Sodom*: "A book like Nietzsche's, for all and none; a book, also, for all time." To me it is Dahlberg's most unsatisfactory, provocative work. He notes that "if this little book appears opaque, the reason is easy to know: the line is gnomic, pulsing with Ovid, Livy, Strabo, Suetonius, Herodian, Plutarch, the Book of Enoch, the Apocalypse of Baruch. The similes themselves are definitions of ancient rituals, which are a bucolic physic for men who feed and gender upon our macadam meadows. The volume is a prayer for a FABLE, and a jot of piercing knowledge regarding Aristotle is that in his old age he found his greatest solace in mythology. Myths are sanctified customs, without which men are morose and slow-witted, and lack the learning to garb themselves suitably, or to bake a good loaf, and build a savory town, —for a people who do not know how to make pleasant bread cannot brew Pramnian wine or amatory verse, as any one who understands the ritualistic occupations of Demeter, Bacchus and Venus may know." In the midst of a welter of modern, arcane parables, there is a central chapter, "The Rational Tree," wherein the book receives any redemption it needs. It is a veritable *Works and Days* in the most ancient tradition, and some of the most resonant language of our time. Just one of innumerable beauties: "Empedokles rests in Asphodels for putting the ass's Bladders in the hills to catch the Etesian gales; Speusippus, inventor of the Twig Basket, frolics with the sea-trulls of Neptune who found the vetch. But Anaximander is in Tartarus tethered to his maps, clocks and gnomon. Who would hesitate to be Virgil or Chaucer rather than Aristotle or Plotinos? Proteus's shells smite the mind more sweetly than Anaxagoras's kosmos, and the Vedic Heifer yields more than Plato's Philosophy."

"Be primordial or decay"—this is the final instruction in Edward Dahlberg's latest work, *The Sorrows of Priapus*. As it was in the beginning, the Paradise of literature, it is a *Works and Days* that evokes a theogony from the writer. But, this is Hesiod, informed by 3000 more years. "Grass and rivers are the pleasures of men which pass away, but the ravines and hills mineral the will." The prose is put together like a rock wall—one oracular, declarative sentence put firmly against another. The result looms above the boneyard of contemporary slovens like the vatic batholith it is. The lichens and stains it bears are exotic ones—Greek natural philosophers, Hebrew prophets, Hakluyt, Monardes, de Vaca, and innumerable mythographers and discoverers. We have a palimpsest of lore from two worlds and five millennia.

Section I, "The Sorrows of Priapus," is an urbane, witty encyclopedia on the physiognomy of a salacious anthropoid *homo sapiens* as he is beset by the ridiculous appetites of his reason, his stomach, and his phallus.

"Most men of considerable intellectual strength have a conspicuous nose resembling a potato, a squill, a testiculate cucumber, for the nose is the second phallus in the male. Besides that, it is the messenger to the testes, for virile olfactories not only take much delight in the *Analects* of Socrates or in the *Dialogues* of Plato, but they also revel in good weather, inhale the seas and fruits, and are very quick to capture the fragrant skin of Nicarete of Megara or the adulterous uterus of Clytemnestra." . . . "Far worse than the human nose, often well-made, and the tongue, are the testes, the most ugly and ill-shaped member. The phallus is a slovenly bag created without intellect or ontological purpose or design, and as long as the human being has this hanging worm appended to his middle, which is no good for anything except passing urine and getting a few miserable irritations, for which he forsakes his mother, his father, and his friends, he will never comprehend the Cosmos." Dahlberg concludes his melancholy but droll prosecution by saying: "Man is at present in a misshapen stage, neither possessing the gentler customs of the beast, nor the faculties of the angel." . . . "Since man is not going to be different for a thousand millenniums he should select certain animals to teach him to be just, eat and gender at regular intervals, and blush." . . . "What is man that he should imagine he is more than a goose?"

In Section II, "The Myth Gatherers" (dedicated to William Carlos Williams of *In the American Grain*), Dahlberg states four postulates for Thermonuclear Pale Face:

1) "Let no one assume that the fables of the red races of the three Americas do not invigorate the intellect. The legends are vast

energies to be domesticated; the continent is a prone mongol Titan, with the jaw of Osiris.

2) "The American intellect is a placeless hunter. It is a negative faculty which devours rather than quiets the heart."

3) "The Indian, or American, mind is primal rather than domestic because it is new. . . ."

4) "Man is at the nadir of his strength when the earth, the seas, the mountains are not in him, for without them his soul is unsourced, and he has no image by which to abide."

Edward Dahlberg's is a tutelary muse. His books seed the mind with desire for other instructive books. Some that come to mind in various ways: Crèvecoeur's *Letters From an American Farmer*, *The Travels of William Bartram*, Henry James' *The American Scene*, D. H. Lawrence's *Studies in Classic American Literature*, Sherwood Anderson's *Many Marriages*, William Carlos Williams' *In the American Grain*, Charles Olson's *Call Me Ishmael*, Josephine Herbst's *New Green World*, and Wright Morris' *The Territory Ahead*. Consciousness is the first problem. Once you've got it, these books suggest where to put it.

Amidst a plethora of oak, maple, streams, hummocks, Pale Face is famished for a tree, a little hill, a foal, a clump of sod; utterly sterile, he begs for the Nature he has warped and killed. He cannot be a thinker, a moral animal, until he returns, as a lover, bringing the peace calumet and the grains of tobacco, as a votive offering, to the cliffs and the wilderness which he threw away.

D. H. LAWRENCE

AN INTRODUCTION TO *BOTTOM DOGS*

WHEN WE THINK of America, and of her huge success, we never realize how many failures have gone, and still go to build up that success. It is not till you live in America, and go a little under the surface, that you begin to see how terrible and brutal is the mass of failure that nourishes the roots of the gigantic tree of dollars. And this is especially so in the country, and in the newer parts of the land, particularly out west. There you see how many small ranches have gone broke in despair, before the big ranches scoop them up and profit by all the back-breaking, profitless, grim labour of the pioneer. In the west you can still see the pioneer work of tough, hard first-comer, individuals, and it is astounding to see how often these individuals, pioneer first-comers who fought like devils against their difficulties, have been defeated, broken, their efforts and their amazing hard work lost, as it were, on the face of the wilderness. But it is these hard-necked failures who really broke the resistance of the stubborn, obstinate country, and made it easier for the second wave of exploiters to come in with money and reap the harvest. The real pioneer in America fought like hell and suffered till the soul was ground out of him: and then, nine times out of ten, failed, was beaten. That is why pioneer literature, which, even from the glimpses one has of it, contains the amazing Odyssey of the brute fight with savage conditions of the western continent, hardly exists, and is absolutely unpopular. Americans will not stand for the pioneer stuff, except in small, sentimentalized doses. They know too well the grimness of it, the savage fight and the savage failure

43

which broke the back of the country but also broke something in the human soul. The spirit and the will survived: but something in the soul perished: the softness, the floweriness, the natural tenderness. How could it survive the sheer brutality of the fight with that American wilderness, which is so big, vast, and obdurate!

The savage America was conquered and subdued at the expense of the instinctive and intuitive sympathy of the human soul. The fight was too brutal. It is a great pity some publisher does not undertake a series of pioneer records and novels, the genuine unsweetened stuff. The books exist. But they are shoved down into oblivion by the common will-to-forget. They show the strange brutality of the struggle, what would have been called in the old language the breaking of the heart. America was not colonized and "civilized" until the heart was broken in the American pioneers. It was a price that was paid. The heart was broken. But the will, the determination to conquer the land and make it submit to productivity, this was not broken. The will-to-success and the will-to-produce became clean and indomitable once the sympathetic heart was broken.

By the sympathetic heart, we mean that instinctive belief which lies at the core of the human heart, that people and the universe itself is *ultimately* kind. This belief is fundamental, and in the old language is embodied in the doctrine: God is good. Now given an opposition too ruthless, a fight too brutal, a betrayal too bitter, this belief breaks in the heart, and is no more. Then you have either despair, bitterness, and cynicism: or you have the much braver reaction which says: God is not good, but the human will is indomitable, it cannot be broken, it will succeed against all odds. It is not God's business to be good and kind, that is man's business. God's business is to be indomitable. And man's business is essentially the same.

This is, roughly, the American position today, as it was the position of the Red Indian when the white man came, and of the Aztec and of the Peruvian. So far as we can make out, neither Redskin nor Aztec nor Inca had any conception of a "good" god. They conceived of implacable, indomitable Powers, which is very different. And that seems to me the essential American position to-day. Of

44

course the white American believes that man should behave in a kind and benevolent manner. But this is a social belief and a social gesture, rather than an individual flow. The flow from the heart, the warmth of fellow-feeling which has animated Europe and been the best of her humanity, individual, spontaneous, flowing in thousands of little passionate currents often conflicting, this seems unable to persist on the American soil. Instead you get the social creed of benevolence and uniformity, a mass *will*, and an inward individual retraction, an isolation, an amorphous separateness like grains of sand, each grain isolated upon its own will, its own indomitableness, its own implacability, its own unyielding, yet heaped together with all the other grains. This makes the American mass the easiest mass in the world to rouse, to move. And probably, under a long stress, it would make it the most difficult mass in the world to hold together.

The deep psychic change which we call the breaking of the heart, the collapse of the flow of spontaneous warmth between a man and his fellows, happens of course now all over the world. It seems to have happened to Russia in one great blow. It brings a people into a much more complete social unison, for good or evil. But it throws them apart in their private individual emotions. Before, they were like cells in a complex tissue, alive and functioning diversely in a vast organism composed of family, clan, village, nation. Now, they are like grains of sand, friable, heaped together in a vast inorganic democracy.

While the old sympathetic glow continues, there are violent hostilities between people, but they are not secretly repugnant to one another. Once the heart is broken, people become repulsive to one another secretly, and they develop social benevolence. They smell in each other's nostrils. It has been said often enough of more primitive or old-world peoples, who live together in a state of blind mistrust but also of close physical connection with one another, that they have no noses. They are so close, the flow from body to body is so powerful, that they hardly smell one another, and hardly are aware at all of offensive human odours that madden the new civilizations. As it says in this novel: The American senses other people by their sweat and their kitchens. By which he means, their repulsive effluvia. And this is basically true. Once the blood-sympathy

45

breaks, and only the nerve-sympathy is left, human beings become secretly intensely repulsive to one another, physically, and sympathetic only mentally and spiritually. The secret physical repulsion between people is responsible for the perfection of American "plumbing," American sanitation, and American kitchens, utterly white-enamelled and antiseptic. It is revealed in the awful advertisements such as those about "halitosis," or bad breath. It is responsible for the American nausea at coughing, spitting, or any of those things. The American townships don't mind hideous litter of tin cans and paper and broken rubbish. But they go crazy at the sight of human excrement.

And it is this repulsion from the physical neighbour that is now coming up in the consciousness of the great democracies, in England, America, Germany. The old flow broken, men could enlarge themselves for a while in transcendentalism, Whitmanish "adhesiveness" of the social creature, noble supermen, lifted above the baser functions. For the last hundred years man has been elevating himself above his "baser functions," and posing around as a transcendentalist, a superman, a perfect social being, a spiritual entity. And now, since the war, the collapse has come.

Man has no ultimate control of his own consciousness. If his nose doesn't notice stinks, it just doesn't, and there's the end of it. If his nose is so sensitive that a stink overpowers him, then again he's helpless. He can't prevent his senses from transmitting and his mind from registering what it does register.

And now, man has begun to be overwhelmingly conscious of the repulsiveness of his neighbour, particularly of the physical repulsiveness. There it is, in James Joyce, in Aldous Huxley, in André Gide, in modern Italian novels like *Parigi*—in all the very modern novels, the dominant note is the repulsiveness, intimate physical repulsiveness of human flesh. It is the expression of absolutely genuine experience. What the young feel intensely, and no longer so secretly, is the extreme repulsiveness of other people.

It is, perhaps, the inevitable result of the transcendental bodiless brotherliness and social "adhesiveness" of the last hundred years. People rose superior to their bodies, and soared along, till they had exhausted their energy in this performance. The energy once exhausted, they fell with a struggling plunge, not down into their bodies again, but into the cess-pools of the body.

The modern novel, the very modern novel, has passed quite away from tragedy. An American novel like *Manhattan Transfer* has in it still the last notes of tragedy, the sheer spirit of suicide. An English novel like *Point Counter Point* has gone beyond tragedy into exacerbation and continuous nervous repulsion. Man is so nervously repulsive to man, so screamingly, nerve-rackingly repulsive! This novel goes one further. Man just *smells*, offensively and unbearably, not to be borne. The human stink.

The inward revulsion of man away from man, which follows on the collapse of the physical sympathetic flow, has a slowly increasing momentum, a wider and wider swing. For a long time the *social* belief and benevolence of man towards man keeps pace with the secret physical repulsion of man away from man. But ultimately, inevitably, the one outstrips the other. The benevolence exhausts itself, the repulsion only deepens. The benevolence is external and extra-individual. But the revulsion is inward and personal. The one gains over the other. Then you get a gruesome condition, such as is displayed in this book.

The only motive power left is the sense of revulsion away from people, the sense of the repulsiveness of the neighbour. It is a condition we are rapidly coming to—a condition displayed by the intellectuals much more than by the common people. Wyndham Lewis gives a display of the utterly repulsive effect people have on him, but he retreats into the intellect to make his display. It is a question of manner and manners. The effect is the same. It is the same exclamation: They stink! My God, they stink!

And in this process of recoil and revulsion, the affective consciousness withers with amazing rapidity. Nothing I have ever read has astonished me more than the "Orphanage" chapters of this book. There I realized with amazement how rapidly the human psyche can strip itself of its awareness and its emotional contacts, and reduce itself to a sub-brutal condition of simple gross persistence. It is not animality—far from it. Those boys are much less than animals. They are cold wills functioning with a minimum of consciousness. The amount that they are *not* aware of is perhaps the

47

most amazing aspect of their character. They are brutally and deliberately unaware. They have no hopes, no desires even. They have even no will-to-exist, for existence even is too high a term. They have a strange, stony will-to-persist, that is all. And they persist by reaction, because they still feel the repulsiveness of each other, of everything, even of themselves.

Of course the author exaggerates. The boy Lorry "Always had his nose in a book"—and he must have got things out of the books. If he had taken the intellectual line, like Mr. Huxley or Mr. Wyndham Lewis, he would have harped on the intellectual themes, the essential feeling being the same. But he takes the non-intellectual line, is in revulsion against the intellect too, so we have the stark reduction to a persistent minimum of the human consciousness. It is a minimum lower than the savage, lower than the African Bushman. Because it is a *willed* minimum, sustained from inside by resistance, brute resistance against any flow of consciousness except that of the barest, most brutal egoistic self-interest. It is a phenomenon, and pre-eminently an American phenomenon. But the flow of repulsion, inward physical revulsion of man away from man, is passing over all the world. It is only perhaps in America, and in a book such as this, that we see it most starkly revealed.

After the orphanage, the essential theme is repeated over a wider field. The state of revulsion continues. The young Lorry is indomitable. You can't destroy him. And at the same time, you can't catch him. He will recoil from everything, and nothing on earth will make him have a positive feeling, of affection or sympathy, or connection.

The tragedian, like Theodore Dreiser and Sherwood Anderson, still dramatizes his defeat and is in love with himself in his defeated rôle. But the Lorry Lewis is in too deep a state of revulsion to dramatize himself. He almost deliberately finds himself repulsive too. And he goes on, just to see if he can hit the world without destroying himself. Hit the world not to destroy it, but to experience in himself how repulsive it is.

Kansas City, Beatrice, Nebraska, Omaha, Salt Lake City, Portland, Oregon, Los Angeles, he finds them all alike, nothing, if not repulsive. He covers the great tracts of prairie, mountain, forest,

48

coast-range, without seeing anything but a certain desert scaliness. His consciousness is resistant, shuts things out, and reduces itself to a minimum.

In the Y.M.C.A. it is the same. He has his gang. But the last word about them is that they stink, their effluvia is offensive. He goes with women, but the thought of women is inseparable from the thought of sexual disease and infection. He thrills to the repulsiveness of it, in a terrified, perverted way. His associates—which means himself also—read Zarathustra and Spinoza, Darwin and Hegel. But it is with a strange, external superficial mind that has no connection with the affective and effective self. One last desire he has—to write, to put down his condition in words. His will-to-persist is intellectual also. Beyond this, nothing.

It is a genuine book, as far as it goes, even if it is an objectionable one. It is, in psychic disintegration, a good many stages ahead of *Point Counter Point*. It reveals a condition that not many of us have reached, but towards which the trend of consciousness is taking us, all of us, especially the young. It is, let us hope, a *ne plus ultra*. The next step is legal insanity, or just crime. The book is perfectly sane: yet two more strides and it is criminal insanity. The style seems to me excellent, fitting the matter. It is sheer bottom-dog style, the bottom-dog mind expressing itself direct, almost as if it barked. That directness, that unsentimental and non-dramatized thoroughness of setting down the under-dog mind surpasses anything I know. I don't want to read any more books like this. But I am glad to have read this one, just to know what is the last word in repulsive consciousness, consciousness in a state of repulsion. It helps one to understand the world, and saves one the necessity of having to follow out the phenomenon of physical repulsion any further, for the time being.

Edward Dahlberg

PREFACE TO *BOTTOM DOGS*, 1961

Tolstoi once said: 'Many men write books, but few are ashamed of them afterwards.'

It was Arabella York, second wife of Richard Aldington, and one of the heroines in *Aaron's Rod*, who sent the MS. of *Bottom Dogs* to D. H. Lawrence. In a letter to me Lawrence spoke of the bony, spartan quality of the novel. I had deliberately expunged some of the joys of this globe, sun, grass, river—the melons and the leeks for which the Israelites pined—in order not to write a slavish book about a society which concealed its filth and cruelty, and that doomed so many of the boys who became vagabonds, pariahs, or hopeless drudges in great cement cities. This sounds a little didactic, but first of all I wanted to tell a story, and maybe I did. But the defect of the novel lies in its jargon.

When I finished *Bottom Dogs* in Brussels and returned to America, I was quite ill in the hospital at Peterborough, New Hampshire. Spite of the tender attention given me by the late widow of the composer, Edward MacDowell, I was slow in recovering. The real malady was *Bottom Dogs*.

There were other authors in Paris in the early twenties, John Hermann and Robert McAlmon, now deceased, who had a passion for what was called the American scene. With all charity to the dead and with very little toward myself, I believe we failed because we thought we could not write about the midwest, Texas or Montana except in the rude American vernacular. There was a great deal of noise about regionalists then who were merely local dunder-

51

heads and yokels of a Main Street intelligentsia. Their creeds were not unlike those held by the Zen Buddhists and others today.

The harm done to the English language has been immense; imagine anyone composing one of the great *Pensées* of Pascal in an abominable tongue; the adages in the *Haiku* are written in a savory language. Spirit is as imponderable as light and the raiment thereof are the lilies or the words that are dearer to us than Solomon's robes. Vile words come from the rabble; wit can be ribald though as well-lettered as Congreve's or Wycherley's plays.

We don't require four-letter words to be erotical, or a whole hogshead of vice to make us pensive. We know all the W.C. pornography anyway, and don't go to books to acquire more sins than we already have. Anyway, sex on the printed page is usually a great bore. Our books are extremely libidinous, and yet we are not amorists. Admitting that we are a licentious band of rebels let us not forget that a little dirt goes a long way.

Plain humble words have more health in them than the latest neologism invented by an advertising scribbler whose sole aim is to sell an adulterated product to a foolish populace. Edmond Goncourt spoke of the craze of originality that had been the curse of literature in his own day. A great deal of the fugitive, humbug vocabulary is what D. H. Lawrence called the American fetish of the wild and the repulsive. Books, like people, are seldom what they seem; do not expect that each volume is the lamb for Abraham, or as Isabella Gardner Tate has it in one of her lovely poems: 'Fathers of Isaacs cease dissembling, Will every thicket yield a ram?'

The other day I was perusing a little essay by Leo Tolstoi on the price of flour which moved me enormously. This is straight, plain writing, I thought. As for the 'spirit of place,' whose significance I scarcely deny, Henry David Thoreau's *Week on the Concord and the Merrimac* or *The Maine Woods* is an American Pisgah. Nor should anyone with great feeling for prose fail to read Herbert Read's *Annals of Innocence and Experience*, the Vergilian Georgics of our times.

Good novels beget warm human books, just as Abraham begat Isaac and Isaac Jacob. I have come to believe that we can be indigenous though we are profoundly affected by Gogol's *Dead Souls* done in a traditional manner, or go to Cobbett's *Rural Rides*, or Thomas Nash's *The Unfortunate Traveler* done in the Elizabethan language of the artisan. I am no foe of the diction of a civilized laborer who does truthful, useful work. Bad or stupid labor produces evil words; what a delight there is in the nautical dialect of Dampier or in the rough, soldierly narrative of Bernal Diaz. What is abominable is the cult of ugliness and the nonsensical credo about being up to date and brand new. Why write savage, loveless books with the vulgar obscenities of a street arab. We have been so determined to destroy the Puritan lechers and all the sexual mania of the social reformers that we find it essential to spew forth every vice in human skin and in words dirtier than Job's muckheap. I once wrote to Sherwood Anderson and told him that *Winesburg, Ohio* was right and that *Bottom Dogs* was wrong because his was warm and human and mine was written in a rough, bleak idiom.

Do we invent poems and novels to be coarser, or to be gravel? Among the Incas hard ground signified a barren heart. The eminent writer, Josephine Herbst, whose volume on John Bartram is a tender gospel of love, has said of *Bottom Dogs*: 'Its limitations set hardened boundaries beyond which Dahlberg was fated to pass or to lose his integral vision in the meaningless violence of typical American fiction. But more like a European writer than any American, he was willing to go down to rot, if need be, in order that he might come up again in a rebirth more central to his vision of an imaginative beyond.' Sibyls or seers we must be so seeded in all ground, European and American, if we are to come up as the glorious flowers of our own new earth, still *terra incognita* to all of us.

Ca'n Peretons
Soller de Mallorca,
España, 1961

WILLIAM CARLOS WILLIAMS

THE FLEA OF SODOM

FOR THE FIRST time in years I was impelled to take down my Bible, to read Jeremiah, and did so—a good thing in itself. The thought of Sir Thomas Browne, the good doctor, came also into my head, *Urne Buriall,* that monumental English, for the book *The Flea of Sodom* is monumental, a small obelisk such as the old people would make. Let me go on talking to myself, there is no call to listen.

I enjoy the book, as far as I've got, and shall continue to read it for the interest I have in it. Why? Because it seems extraordinarily truthful in its observation of types found in the New York literary slums. Contemptuous of them, while at the same time the overwhelming loneliness of the "I" of the journal, for it is a journal of daily happenings, is so bitterly lonesome that he has to go sit on the steps before the door of those he hates. They are to him at least alive, at least aware that salesmanship is not virtue.

But that is only the account of what happens, a merely going from one street to another within a compass of five or six streets, an area no larger than the agora or that of ancient Jerusalem. It may be that this limiting of the scene of a philosophic statement to a small area of images, a few 5th class restaurants is the perfect way to handle the city and what is to be said of it. It is the size of an Athens, even a Rome of the effective precincts.

The whole story takes place in a few city blocks. Yes, but what language is it written in? It may seem at first like some esoteric jargon but that's not true. There are a few archaisms such as "carnal tides," "flayed my head for psalms," but in general the words are those of the newspaper.

55

What is it then that gives the archeologic flavor? The names of the actors. Pilate Agenda, Ephraim Bedlam, Ajax Proletcult, Thais Colette, Andromache (her mother was black) Golem, Monsieur Golem Patron.

Nothing happens! But it is because nothing can happen. They are all dead, both the living and the dead are dead. So we see no more than the shades shuffling back and forth among the New York streets, wearing now rags, now mink coats—while the *dechirée*, the torn "I," is shunned even by the dead who try to escape from him by exiting through another door or sneaking down an alley. Often they try to buy him off with half a dozen bars of nut chocolate which he finds too late were only a ruse.

The flavor of the Bible dominates the place just as it does the movements of the Salvation Army. Christ stands visibly above a motley crowd. There is no concession to pederasts or Communists, heavy jawed women or   .   a liar is a liar and the coward is a coward. All the petty meannesses of the smug-faced world of money and "art" is thrown into the same swill bucket—where it belongs. No exceptions are admitted.

Lazarus, I am Lazarus! Embarrassing, undemanding, forgiving. The sniggling artists who ridicule him are cursed in archaic terms; he is futile, tormented, ineffective. It is the dregs that will not be destroyed but cry out, smoke from the fire.

In the face of today's fear, in the presence of Pilate Agenda, the eternal Lazarus is snugged and avoided, Andromache (whose mother was colored) Golem, Monsieur Golem—Lazarus with a parched mouth insulted by children and artistic pansies, unstuffed female perverts psychologically excused for their double genitals   . crawls about the city slums, hated and alone   .   in breakbone English to resemble the slow accretions of a Sir Thomas Browne.

How shall he be avoided? How can we accept him—he'll never go away if we let him in. He'll want to get under our clean blankets with his dirty feet. His humility is disgusting, a man such as that ought to work. He could get a job, even dishwashing—except there's a union. He is poverty stricken because he psychologically WANTS to be that way. It is a kind of vanity to be dirty, even to be sick. We certainly can't have him here.

If he doesn't do any worse he'll talk us to death. We haven't the time for him. We've got work to do. Or let him stand on a picket line somewhere. Ideologically he OUGHT to be on a picket line,   .

at least that's what we used to think Communism stood for. Apparently it doesn't. If a man won't work he shouldn't expect to eat. Personally, I think he ought to be shot. Is he a Jew? Hitler was right after all. Or is it Stalin? Or is or was Henry Ford the genius of the age? Disgusting. How can a man work toward a decent world. Jesus wept.

The Flea of Sodom. What is the flea of Sodom? We are Sodom, Lazarus is the flea. Miserable as he is, but elusive as a flea, small, easily crushed between the nails, he will return to the end of time to pester us with his insistences. I remember the disgust of a friend on hearing a priest speak of lice as the pearls of the poor. I know now what she meant.

This is Dahlberg's insistence, his agony. He likens himself to a flea to rouse the sodomites that occupy the city to wake at night and   .   and   Democrats and Communists, both at fault, both winking the plight of the world.

It is a moral we must heed. Economics we think are male and female, virtue is a divided asset, one for you and another for me, with Lazarus' face (Perhaps Lazarus is a genius and may be the one to make a better airplane; think!) watching us from the gutter.

Is this style ancient, unworthy of our attention? Is it too hard? Why did he write that way? (Because the agony is old, long told in a dead language.) But the occasion is still there. We CANNOT avoid it. We have never avoided it. We have only alighted it, turned and run. It is there, it is there and is not won by being this or that. We shift right, we shift left—it is no good. We welch the facts. More than the facts we welch the human being.

I don't see how Dahlberg could have written what he has to say differently. It is a timeless, a half-rotten language, it is a voidless language. This isn't a tract. It's a work of ant-like manufacture. It is painful, tight—it creeps on small nimble legs to build its small house that any passing foot wipes out and in a moment it has begun again to build. It will not stop building. It will build out of sand, small stones. It is the insect of love.

57

Dahlberg is a terrifying person, the most annoying person possibly to be found because he cannot be ignored. He despises the suave language that is used for the blather of our slickness. He wants us to be aware of the difficulties; he is making a thing, a replica, as the maimed make a replica of a lost limb to hang in a chapel where they go for relief and comfort. Only Dahlberg is making a replica for the whole man, the whole man beset by panaceas called economics, politics of whatever color, whatever fabric. Until the man himself has been heeded nothing can go forward.

He speaks of a fable, of an image, of the need for myth. If we only knew how sadly the myth of man himself is neglected. We are images of despair, all our politics is an image of despair. We need sthenic images, the imagination, the rekindling imagination is a foible, it is a fluid, as true as the fluid that generates the child itself.

I am conscious as I read of all sorts of references as I go along. I do not believe that the names are emptily put down; I find references to the classics, to the Bible, to our own past, and I do not know exactly what they signify. This is a great barrier to understanding —but I accept it.

I have been speaking so far of "The Flea of Sodom," Part 1. Part 2, "The Rational Tree," is something else. There a more sanguine mood rises and the scene, a dialectic! A new place like that of Fray Luis on his island in the Tagus with his brother priests. "Good towns grow up by Bacchus yews on warm-nymphed seas twined in Poseidon's kelpy trident." This is a quieter world. Tho' no winning one.

What winds drive the modern Ishmael   .   .   Call me Ishmael, cries Herman Melville. Melville and Dahlberg have much in common toward the world, a voluptuousness which is back of their complaining, a richness. Warm livered Jews   etc.

He appears learned in the classics—Virgil Verberus—Cerberus is alive. He exists as much today as ever in the old myths. The myths are thus proven true, not myths at all because they still reflect our world. They ARE. It is true. We are contemporary with the past if unworthy of it.

He is for no side, no party. Is he for man himself, the vile that permits such vomit to be eaten as we eat day by day? We are lost in the face of limitless that is present time, we are .   contemptible.

Ishmael hungers for man. The first book is Jeremiah. This book is New Testament; it is sadly sanguine, almost a tone of The Song in reverse. A longing for talk, for companionship, for a mere touch .   banished by the Politbureau and the U.S. Treasury.

"The fool and the Troglodite Onan feign a weariness with friendship and speech." Unhappily they do not feign it, they have it formidably within them in the form of hurry and business. They have been frightened, frightened by both sides that this is necessary to live. To what? What? Is this living?

This is not a narrative as the first book is but a thesis, an agonized complaint.

Dahlberg is a Rabbi gone up beyond doctrine into a world sphere who would have every day the Sabbath.

II: The Rational Tree

—is irrational in a surface sense but, admitting incongruences, inconsistencies, and incompatibilities, it presents a truth: It seems to me, as far as I can make it out, a forwarding of Hebraic culture as against the Hellenic on which Christendom is, paradoxically, founded. Was not Jesus' father, as Hegel convincingly argues from the complection of his thought, in fact a Greek?

Your Greeks, said the Egyptian priest .   Solon, Solon, said an Egyptian priest, your Greeks are all boys. We too are boys in Christendom .   loving games more than thought. In which we excel and may die for it, as the Hebrews, who think, will not. That may be our fate. —and foolish partisans: the virtues, we think, are southern virtues or northern virtues and wisdom either western or eastern. We are governed by the points of the compass, apparently, more than by our minds or even our interests.

But all through it runs fear, fear that drives us to the homosexual out of dread of our fathers. Love must be either philosophical or sexual, we cannot understand that it is both—that when we say

59

"love" neither is excluded. The "hot livered" Jews do not, says Dahlberg, make that typically Platonic mistake. It is the generative and of the generative, for without generation *the* generation ceases.

Animals abound in "The Rational Tree": little culture lives far from the spring (about which the agora was always clustered) or the horse trough: The horse is about all that remains clean in the world, he quotes Swift as saying.

The Muses' fount or Rachel's well—receive great praise at his hands against the destroying iron of what has since happened to the world.

His reading appears to be enormous, from the Upanishads through the Hebraic, the Latin and Chaucer to Melville and the newsprint of the day.

I'd like to quote p. 82 entire as the best in the book.

Legends tutor the spirit and quiet the race, but metaphysics wears away the mind.

This, "The Rational Tree," is far and away the better book—as between the narrative and the next. I find it extremely satisfying, better given, fuller of wisdom and better written. It is often brilliant in its symposiums of past learning. A sweetness that the first lacks.

It is a sweet book, as a nut is sweet, compared with the bitterness of the first. I wonder which was written first.

False bread and a rabble literature and town go together

—none who has eaten of the rational fruit may know the Tree of Life   :   Eden.

October 13

The last words in the book are, " 'O my Bitterness, I am the SHAME Crying out of the Ground.' " They are the last words of 3 parables, for a friend   .   3 artificial flowers   resembling nothing that is real, for the reason, that to a man seeking "the truth" even the flowers, which we call flowers, are shameful because they reflect our lives. Our lives are shameful, shameful so that everything we have touched or so much as looked at is defiled. We must be born again   .

Dahlberg denies criticism, he is lower than "understanding"

.   I don't know how even to speak of the book. I want to say that he touches a man BENEATH experience, he strikes DOWN through the mind to a nature that is so long buried by our civilities that it is rotten   .   We can't even resurrect it, it is so long buried.

Yet it is what we are. It is ourselves   .   far past knowledge. It is so far past knowledge that it is mouldy, as secret as what we knew was a life because we see the evidence of it in Mayan temples but we cannot resurrect it.

But he makes us realize that what he is seeking to resurrect and does describe in bitterest terms is OURSELVES. We cannot understand him because he is telling us about ourselves.

I doubt that his words have any other specific sense. I at least cannot find a syllabus. It can't be there. It is shocking when suddenly he says "Charles Olson." It is shocking because the name of an actual, living person makes us realize that up to that moment we have been in some region we have not (recently) inhabited. Some unearthed place   .   where we were extraordinarily alone, half decayed

.   and yet we had once lived there and gone off   .
yet it is our home.

In "The Wheel of Sheol" he inveighs against ever having left that home   .   of the prophets. "Beliar" (is it Be Liar)
liars that we are every moment of our lives. Is it some *place*, some lost place of infancy, Dahlberg's infancy that we know was lost and to which he wants violently to return?

But it is an identification between the SHAME of our lives and that deeply buried past which is "virtue," "happiness," all that is desirable.

He makes us realize something only the prophets know, what beauty is possible to the earth   .   to us: a far removed past. An allegory, a semi-historical allegory   .   a Faery Queen
in a new dress

The horrible welding of an iron rim upon the fiery wheel to drive it cursing the world   .

"Bellerophon"   .   what words! It has the disordered imagery that distinguishes Isaiah. A blast against "the dream." A vast

61

apostrophe   .   against the intellect   "a pitiless, artful, ravening beast."

and so we have   —   the whole book is subhuman, unintelligible   —   refusing to be human, refusing to acknowledge analysis   —

refusing to compromise with man   as he has become. It is the same drive that will not say "I" but "i"   .   but raised to the most uncompromising power

and so we have
1. a narrative
2. an essay
3. an allegory
4. an apostrophe
5. parables

SIR HERBERT READ

THE SORROWS OF PRIAPUS

THIS BOOK is very graciously dedicated to me, which might preclude, in the conventional ethics of reviewing, any comment on my part. But the book is exceptional, and the occasion is exceptional; I shall not hesitate, therefore, to declare my opinion, which is based on friendship only to the extent that friendship brings with it sympathy and understanding. I have followed Edward Dahlberg's career since the publication of his first book, *Bottom Dogs*, which D. H. Lawrence so perspicaciously fathered; and I have watched his long struggle for recognition with anxious dismay. There is no greater reflection on the blindness and injustice of American criticism than the obstinate refusal of any considerable public to admit the genius of this writer. It is true that the critics, and the great American public whom they serve, have some grounds for reluctance or resentment. Edward Dahlberg has been and still is an excoriating flagellator of every element in their civilization. Even in this book he tells us that "Pale Face is famished for a tree, a little hill, a foal, a clump of sod; utterly sterile, he begs for the Nature he has warped and killed. He cannot be a thinker, a moral animal, until he returns, as a lover, bringing the peace calumet and the grains of tobacco, as a votive offering, to the cliffs and wilderness which he threw away."

One cannot read two sentences, such as these, without being aware that one is in the presence of a writer who is reanimating the English language, cleansing it of the lazy sludge of loose thought and impoverished feeling, lifting it high above the con-

63

taminating sewage of the daily press. This book is the pure music of words. Each paragraph is as composed as a prelude of Bach's, as visually organized, as to its images, as a painting by Piero della Francesca. Does this make for easy reading? The answer is No, for all great art is a discipline, and demands the concentration we would give, were we blessed with belief, to ritual and celebration. The reward is to that extent the greater: the flooding of the mind with wonder, with harmony, with what on occasions I have called "the sense of glory."

The obvious comparisons are with those supreme masters of the English music, Sir Thomas Browne and Robert Burton. But Dahlberg has also the geographical imagination of a Milton, and the moral fervor of a Montaigne. The first quality enriches his style with the jewelry of place-names, which are so significant because they are the fruit of an original intercourse between man's mind and his environment:

> The Inca was a Theban of the Andes; the first Inca came out of a crag at *Paucartampu.* The peaks of mountains were his *huacas* or idols; he venerated the Sierras and the Punas and his grief was dry. Rocks are the herbals of sun races. Medusa is less of a marvel than the hot fountain in the *Guancauilca* in Peru which, as it pours forth, turns into pebbles. Stones are the remedies for the grieving mind and the flesh which are water and grass. Grass and rivers are the pleasures of men which pass away, but the ravines and hills mineral the will. The Egyptian embalmers at Heliopolis turned the head of the deceased away from the River Nile. The *Chotas* of Mexico worship the dawn and stones; *Tohil,* the god who gave the *Quiché Maya* fire by shaking his sandals, was of obsidian origin. The primal gods sprang up from an aerolite that had fallen from the skies.

Must one pause to analyze such a passage, in the manner of a college seminarist? To point out the assonances, the cadences, the vital variety of the rhythms? Or the condensed observation and wisdom of such sentences as "Rocks are the herbals of sun races"? And this is a passage chosen at random. *Every* paragraph of these hundred and twenty pages has a similar felicity, until one begins to

64

read them as the stanzas of an epic are read, to linger at each step of the soaring structure.

This book, as I have said, is also a morality—not an ethical treatise, which would imply a logical argument, but a discourse studded with apothegms. The book has two parts, roughly equal: the first, "The Sorrows of Priapus," concerned with the mysteries of sex, as revealed in the Hebraic and Hellenistic traditions; the second, "The Myth Gatherers" (dedicated to William Carlos Williams), seeking chthonic roots for an American tradition in pre-Columbian history. It is difficult to see how two such disparate themes can be related; but they face each other like the leaves of a triptych, and the final paragraph of the first part, and the first paragraph of the final part, unite the leaves with golden hinges:

In Eden there are two trees: "Behold, I have set before thy face life and death, good and evil: choose life." Every Prophet has perished, for if man eat of the Tree of Knowledge he will die, and the Angel with the flaming sword that guards the Tree of Life can never be overcome until men are of a different shape, substance and mind . . . Many stars will dim, and planets go to their doom, and oceans sorrow, before the human race can attain one sublime identity. When the two-headed animal that writes strays from the haunts of Artemis, the river gods, and the precincts of Thoth, he is the lawless goat.

The modern American has thus strayed from the haunts of Artemis, like a lawless goat, and now:

Man is always seeking Eden, and the geographers of Paradise have named the rivers and located the blessed ground where Adam and Babylonian Gilgamesh dwelt. In the beginning there were cockle, scoriae, sea lava; the onyx, jacinth, emerald of Elysium resemble Ecbatna, the summer site of Semiramis, rather than the primordial earth of the crustacea that inhabited the great waters. When nature wears scoriae and igneous rock, she is the maiden, and her matrix is holy.

The continent of America is such a holy matrix, but its conquerors were overcome by its "wild, vast weight." All the poetry of this epic struggle is condensed and crystallized in these sixty pages, and the prophecy ends with the command: "Be primordial or decay."

65

One returns to the first part of the book, because it is more difficult—difficult to understand and accept. The word "prophet" must be used deliberately to describe this writer: he writes in the spirit of Esdras, whose *Book* he quotes: "The stroke of the tongue breaketh the bones." Like the prophets, he is puritanical, which does not mean anti-sexual. Rather he would purify sex from its lewd abuses. "Men learned to copulate from the angels that entered the daughters of men, and their issue were giants, who, being amorous beasts with human parts, were confused and stupid, because it is the mind in man that baffles the animal in him." Always this insistence on the mind, as the sole justification of living. "Man is at present in a misshapen stage, neither possessing the gentler customs of the beast, nor the faculties of the angel."

What is the ultimate form or the divine shape of future man? The author asks this question and suggests that "the highest man will have no scrotum; it is ludicrous for a moral philosopher to scrape and scratch as any worm"; but concludes nevertheless that "it is impossible to predict the metamorphosis of human beings." "Man is water and parched land; fire and rock are his hopes; desire is the Trade Wind; the fruit of the Tucuma palm is the Arcadia of the macaws, and the ruse of mortals. . . . Be primordial or decay."

I hope I have given sufficient grounds for the suggestion that *The Sorrows of Priapus*, like *Leaves of Grass*, or *Moby Dick*, is an authentic and rare contribution to the formation or elucidation of an American myth. "A book for brave readers and poets," as the author himself claims. But it is also, in its physical presentation, a book for those who consider that the book itself can be a work of art. The text is accompanied by forty-two drawings by a great American artist, sensitive drawings, fantastic images, conceived by Ben Shahn. They constitute a perfect illumination of this legendary book, this American bestiary or missal, and Elaine Lustig has coordinated text and illustrations in a perfect layout. There is a limited edition of one hundred and fifty copies on mouldmade Arches paper; the letterpress has been composed and printed by the Thistle Press; the binding is by the Russell-Rutter Company. A noble book has a noble shape.

JOSEPH EVANS SLATE

EDWARD DAHLBERG'S MORAL BOOK

OF EROTIC BEASTS

WHEN *The Sorrows of Priapus* was published in 1957, its full significance could not have been grasped, even by Dahlberg's most devoted readers. In 1967 it appears more and more to be a key to all of his work since *The Flea of Sodom,* a way to open up the inner relationships between Dahlberg's prose style, his regard for literary convention, and his unfashionable concept of art. In the first half of *The Sorrows of Priapus,* which might be called "The Moral Book of Erotic Beasts," these angles meet in the archetypal analogy of man with animal that is announced in the first sentence of Chapter I: "Man must be classed among the brutes, for he is still a very awkward and salacious biped." Classifying and the climactic word *biped* suggest immediately a "scientific" approach to the central analogy, identifying the work to follow as a bestiary.

The bestiary written and read today is most likely to be an "Animal ABC," "A Visit to the Zoo," a "Noah's Ark" or some similar children's book. A few of these, such as George Macbeth's riddling *Noah's Journey* (1966), are the serious work of serious poets, but the high form of the bestiary commonly lacks clear connections with the popular or subliterary form, so that the monolithic bestiary of ancient and medieval tradition has today split into two pieces, of which the low is by far the larger fragment. Because such popular bestiaries are thoroughly conventional, however, they bring up into clear relief the fundamental patterns of the bestiary, the

67

conventions which Dahlberg, in his disgust with "originality," chose to work within.

At its lowest, the popular bestiary is a collection of pictures with captions, pictures of animals with their names. In this rudimentary form, the bestiary satisfies naively scientific desires to connect pictures or names—images or signs of natural things—with the things themselves. I call this scientific because it follows the intellectual route of anyone using the models constructed by science to understand the natural world. Accordingly, the reader of a bestiary, who has historically been someone viewing it as a useful model of the natural world, is a reader of science; the writer of a bestiary, traditionally thinking of himself as a model-maker, is a scientist. Aristotle's *Historia Animalium*, Pliny's *Naturalis Historia*, the *Physiologus* of the middle ages, Buffon's gigantic *Histoire naturelle*, Fabre's *Souvenirs entomologiques*, all attest how long the bestiary has been a medium of scientific thought.

The genre is traditionally rational and scientific, yet it is misleading to assert, as T. H. White does in *The Bestiary: A Book of Beasts* (1954), that this is the way in which a twelfth-century bestiary can and ought to be read today. This is like expecting a child's animal book, useful to the child who merely wanted the names of things, to remain useful through the child's adult life. Confronted with a medieval bestiary, the modern reader with little or no sense of the whole tradition must inevitably find it a poor model and reject it as scientifically useless or read it imaginatively as a work of art. To do either would be a mistake. Properly, the bestiary should be read as both art and science, as "new" and unique work and as part of a very old tradition of scientific writing. Its unicorns may be understood imaginatively, but a knowledge of unicorns, one should remember, was not always considered useless. Even when its scientific bias is obscured by theological fogs or invalidated by time, the bestiary retains enough of this tradition to affect its essential qualities as art. Even in the twentieth century, the bestiary is always to some extent useful, always didactic.

Today didactic works are usually dismissed as non-art; the "pure" concepts of art still dominate our minds. Nevertheless, didactic theories of art cannot be finally dismissed, as Dahlberg sug-

68

gests. His use of the bestiary forces us to go back to much older views, to question the assumptions of the last one-hundred and fifty years. And it is not surprising that this doubt of the assumptions behind modern art underlies all Dahlberg's criticism in *Truth is More Sacred*. There he associates the ancients with the memories of our origins and the moderns with forgetting the history of man's beginnings: "Homer never wrote personal memoirs, like the novels of Flaubert, Proust, Lawrence, James, Joyce. This is an occupation for the lagging ear, and for the garrulous mind, not for a potent intellect." Because they forget, they lack a sense of traditional wisdom and traditional form; they would not understand the tradition of the bestiary which makes it not only didactic but also moralistic.

The bestiary is moralistic to the extent that it is emblematic. The bestiary traditionally connects words with pictures, and this is true of both high and low forms today. Children's books are unthinkable without pictures, while the best-known French bestiaries of this century created such strong ties to the graphic arts that Picasso in 1942 invoked the name of Buffon when he wished to name a series of animal lithographs. He undoubtedly knew Raoul Dufy's woodcuts accompanying Apollinaire's *Le Bestiaire* (1911) and the prints provided by Toulouse-Lautrec and Bonnard for Renard's *Histoires naturelles* in 1899 and 1904. The drawings by Ben Shahn which appear in *The Sorrows of Priapus* are in the same tradition: as graphic art, the pictures assert the right of the book to be considered a serious modern bestiary; as emblems, the pictures suggest the conventional character of the text, the moral function which it has in common with the illuminated bestiaries of the middle ages.

By literary convention, *emblem* means a picture with a motto or set of verses intended as a moral lesson. Emblem books were common in renaissance Europe but apparently did not survive to the present in any recognizable form, unless in the trademarks and slogans of modern advertising. Because *emblematic* traditionally implies moral allegory, it is usually contrasted with *symbolistic*, which implies interpretation on several levels besides the allegorical. The limitations of the emblem are obvious: single-level reference produces a thin-textured work that also lacks subtlety, while

69

the specialization of the emblem—compared with the image or the symbol—produces a metaphor so static and isolated that it fits only into discontinuous structures. The first limitation means that an emblematic work such as a bestiary must remain didactic or run the risk of losing its identity. (The only exception is parody where the traditional form is retained in order to ridicule its didacticism— Hilaire Belloc's *Bad Child's Book of Beasts* is a good example.)

The second limitation means that a bestiary, as an emblematic work, is a discontinuous genre, a structure of separate, isolated, unmoving parts. It lacks both the articulated structure of logical writing and the narrative structure of fiction. And as the history of the bestiary shows, discontinuity has periodically forced the genre to make temporary alliances with a kind of literature having either logical or narrative connections between parts. For example, Richard de Fournival's thirteenth-century *Bestiaire d'amour* contains all the animals and pictures one might expect, but these appear within an unexpected logical structure. To persuade Richard's lady of his love, the separate units have been connected and the whole work given a kind of coherence quite distinct from the discontinuity of the conventional bestiary. Although the zoological information, such as the pelican who gives his heart's blood to those he has slain and the raven who attacks a dead man first at the eyes, remains basically the same, the discontinuous has quickly been converted into something more closely allied to the writer's purposes.

On the other side from logic and rhetoric, the discontinuous bestiary has shown even greater attraction for narrative structure, conducting a long affair with the beast fable. The whole work may be given a narrative structure, in the manner that the title of *Noah's Journey* clearly implies; or, the life of each animal may be narrated and the emblematic description become a parable. All medieval accounts of the elephant included the information that a fallen elephant could be raised only by the aid of a certain species of small elephant. This almost never remained a discontinuous fact, but instead became related to other facts in a narrative form, as a metrical version of the *Physiologus*, written by Bishop Theobald in the eleventh century, demonstrates:

70

When it desires to sleep, or recover by slumber when wearied,
It finds a fairly large tree, 'gainst which it leans its great bulk,
This tree the hunter observes, then cutting half through it, remains there,
Hidden, he then keeps his watch, till when the beast seeks its sleep,
Thinking its safety secure in the usual shade of its own tree,
Comes there, and leaning thereon, falls with the fall of the tree.
If the man should not be there, it will groan long and lastly will trumpet,
Elephants, many and great, quickly then come to its help,
This one, unable to rise, they all join in trumpeting loudly,
Suddenly comes to their aid, one of them smallest of all,
Of whom, 'tis strange to relate, its instinct now raises the fallen,
Who, in this manner, escapes snares, which the hunter has laid.

As a Christian parable, the interpretation of this is of course predictable:

Thus Adam first of the race was the cause of man's fall in the garden,
Whom Moses wishing to raise, all of his efforts were vain,
After him prophets desired to do the same work, but they could not,
Then to men's aid came the Christ. Himself the answer to prayers,
Who being humble and small, since God took the shape of the human,
Thus he lifted men up, making Himself the accused. . . .

Despite the commonness of parables and other divergent parts in individual bestiaries, the bestiary as a genre had no difficulty in retaining its integrity. It traditionally shared with the beast fable a vision of creation in which nature mirrored humanity, but it stood apart rather clearly because of its inherent didacticism and its discontinuous structure. With such a primitively repetitious form, too, the bestiary was never far from ritual, the conventionally repeated

71

action whose meaning is embodied in myth. In the simplicity of the genre and its unity of myth, ritual and literary convention, the bestiary could not have been bettered as a medium for conveying in its own terms the importance of myth. And Dahlberg must also have seen the opportunities the structure offered for interrelations with the herbal, the theogony, and the fable.

The ritual performed in the bestiary is the naming of the animals, the action by which Adam symbolically participated in the creation. (In Genesis, the naming immediately precedes the creation of Eve, another action in which God and man, so to speak, collaborate.) Then, before the Deluge, Noah repeated Adam's ritual, both to help create a new world and to insure connections with the old, antediluvian world. Although the ritual may also assert man's separation from the lower creatures and celebrate his authority over them, thus exalting man as scientist, the need to play the role of creator obviously has priority today. For twentieth-century writers like Dahlberg, the ritual of creation, in which reader and writer join in the figure of Adam, Noah, or Orpheus, represents deeper human needs and more basic desires. Beneath the level at which an "Animal ABC" operates as primitive science, lies hidden a level at which it operates as mythic renewal, a way of going back to racial beginnings and seeing all creation as it was on the sixth day.

Just as twentieth-century painting not only returned to basic forms and primitive values but also went back to its roots in new uses of conventional subject matter, Guillaume Apollinaire returned to virtually everything that was basic, primitive and conventional in the bestiary in 1911. In *Le Bestiaire, ou Cortège d'Orphée*, Apollinaire brought the bestiary up to date by emphasizing its unsophisticated formal qualities, its emblematic nature, and its mythic possibilities. In "L'Elephant," for example, he exploits the primitive simplicity of rhythm, line and stanza, develops a single point of comparison (or at least appears to), and makes the speaker of the lines Orphée, who relates them directly to his work as poet:

> Comme un éléphant son ivoire
> J'ai en bouche un bien précieux.
> Pourpre mort? . . . J'achète ma gloire
> Aux prix des mots mélodieux.

It is easy to understand why this sequence of poems is often credited with reviving the bestiary in our time. But its fame in this historical sense is not fully deserved, for it made little use of the didactic aspect of the genre and no use of the scientific associations at all. Furthermore, it could not begin a modern tradition which was already under way in French prose before 1908.

When prose became the language of science after the middle ages, it was inevitable that most serious or high forms of the bestiary would be written in prose; by the end of the nineteenth century, consequently, prose was established as part of the tradition of the bestiary. From this point of view, Apollinaire's *Bestiaire* in verse avoids a difficult formal problem by merely skipping over the age of scientific prose and returning to the middle ages. In the long run, Apollinaire also emphasizes so many low or popular forms of the bestiary that his work is less relevant to Dahlberg's than that of Jules Renard and Rémy de Gourmont, who both wrote high or serious bestiaries in prose.

The title of Renard's *Histoires naturelles* (1896) ironically alludes to Buffon's great encyclopedic work in forty-four volumes, for Renard's is a small book whose most obvious characteristic is extreme concision. In fact, Renard's descriptions are so concise that they almost never repeat the name of the animal; some do not even contain a pronoun referring to the subject. The cockroach is simply "Noir et collé comme un trou de serrure"; the flea is "Un grain de tabac à ressort." Others are isolated exclamations: the grass snake (La Couleuvre) evokes "De quel ventre est-elle tombée, cette colique?" and the green lizard, "Prenez garde à la peinture!" When Renard calls himself "le chasseur d'images," he emphasizes another difference from the natural scientist: rather than constructing a model by which he can control the natural world, the artist is hunting its very essence and—because he often fails—destroying what he seeks to grasp. And finally, the plural *histoires* in the title contradicts any idea of a unified natural history; here the discontinuous structure of the bestiary resists the pressure to imitate the connected discourse of nineteenth-century science.

Renard's *images* are brief glimpses of nature in the form of prose poems, obviously not *histoires* in the sense of narratives. Yet he

73

flirts with the didactic as one might expect: as Toulouse-Lautrec noted in his design for the book cover, his name is that of the animal hero of so many beast fables, and he is almost irresistibly drawn by his material. In one microcosmic piece, finally called "Singes" but separately published under the title "Fantasies parisiennes: Nos bêtes," Renard satirizes the visitor to the zoo who can only see the animals in human terms:

Allez voir le yack lourd de pensées préhistoriques; la girafe qui nous montre, par-dessus les barreaux de la grille, sa tête au bout d'une pique; l'éléphant qui traîne ses chaussons devant sa porte, courbé, le nez bas: il disparaît presque dans le sac d'une culotte trop remontée, et, derrière, un petit bout de corde pend.

Allez donc voir le por-épic garni de porte-plume bien gênants pour lui et son amie; le zèbre, modèle à transparent de tous les autres zèbres; la panthère descendue au pied de son lit; l'ours qui nous amuse et ne s'amuse guère, et le lion qui bâille, à nous faire bâiller.

In this passage Renard catches himself being didactic but can't help it; the form insists and his desire to lose himself in nature rouses him to react to this scene of too easy humanizing of beasts. In "Une Famille d'arbres," he longs to belong to a family of trees in order to escape the burden of human feeling and memory, the pangs of which are sharpest when he thinks of his own family.

By his title and by his use of prose, Renard places his work in the scientific tradition while treating it ironically, as Dahlberg was to do fifty years later. Unlike Dahlberg, however, he also treats the unavoidable didacticism of the genre ironically. Unable to exploit the didactic element fully because he held a basically "pure" concept of art, Renard resembles Apollinaire rather than Dahlberg or Rémy de Gourmont.

In 1903 Rémy de Gourmont published a bestiary unqualifiedly didactic. Furthermore, his *Physique de l'amour, essai sur l'instinct sexuel,* translated by Ezra Pound as *The Natural Philosophy of Love* (1922), seems to have little relationship to either literature or imaginative life. It does not even appear to belong to the bestiary tradition unless we recognize the eighteenth-century natural histories and entomologies as part of the full history of the genre.

Although many of Gourmont's facts clearly come from the *Souvenirs entomologiques*, an autobiographical treatment of the lives of insects by his contemporary Henri Fabre, he more often refers to the ideas of the eighteenth-century naturalists who, he believes, should have been rational enough to see the meaning of the sexual habits of animals. Gourmont states—in Pound's words—that "man is the sum of the animals, the sum of their instincts," though the Church has long persuaded us that man belongs to a different creation entirely. To carry on the rational enquiries of the eighteenth century to their logical conclusions, is to destroy their falsehoods and at the same time return man to the sanity of the animals and insects. Gourmont suggests without irony that the morality of the natural world should be extended to man:

> There are species in which the position of the organs is such that the same individual cannot be at the same time the female for whom he acts as male, but he can at that moment serve as female to another male, who is female to a third, and so on. This explains the garlands of spintrain gasteropodes which one sees realizing innocently and according to the ineluctable wish of nature, carnal imaginations that have been the boast of erotic humanity. Facing this light from animal habits, debauchery loses all character and all its tang, because it loses all immorality. Man, who unites in himself the aptitudes of all the animals, could not escape the heritage of their sexual methods; and there is no lewdness which has not its normal type in nature, somewhere.

La Physique de l'amour is not only strongly didactic but fully traditional in seeing all creation as emblematic, though Gourmont's moralizing is anti-religious. He cites the beast fable *Roman du Renart* as an accurate source of information about families of foxes, although he rejects the stories of the sexual shyness of elephants as wholly legendary and thinks that Fabre mistook sadism for maternal devotion in the case of a certain bee-killing wasp. (A theme of female physical superiority, cruelty and betrayal, specifically related to Baudelaire's giantess, runs through the book.) He objects to the conclusions of religious moralists, but chiefly because of their selectivity, not to their moralizing:

75

Moralists love bees from whom they distill examples and aphorisms. They recommend us work, order, economy, foresight, obedience and divers virtues other. Abandon yourself to labor: Nature wills it. Nature wills everything. She is complacent to all the activities; to our imaginings there is no analogy which she will refuse, not one.

Examples, in this context, mean moral parables like most beast fables; Gourmont offers as an alternative to them the scientific bestiary with his own a-moralizing. He is no less eager than the medieval monk to go beyond the facts of zoology and entomology, so he insists finally on the morality of nature, restricted only by the limits of man's intelligence.

To Gourmont, man is monstrous because he is unlike the other animals: his intelligence "immeasurably surpasses his organs, and submerges them; it demands of them the impossible and the absurd." In sexual acts the human brain demands of the organs more than they are able to give, so although mankind's practices are the sum of all the beasts' sexual diversity, individual man is a monster doomed to unhappiness. This conflict between the rational and the instinctual is merely one of the sorrows of Priapus, that monstrously absurd figure of erotic man created by Edward Dahlberg.

Invoking the muse in appropriately classical accents before opening the "Moral Book of Erotic Beasts," Dahlberg begins "Sing Venus Hetaera." As Eve, the source of his sorrows, to Priapus' Adam, Aphrodite the Strumpet embodies two views of sex simultaneously: Aphrodite is human sexuality seen wisely and mythically through the best minds of the past; the Strumpet is simply a personification of bestial lust, sex seen myopically by men without the traditional wisdom of myth. Priapus was never much more than a crude, lustful monster, but Aphrodite retains some marks of her former significance, some traces of the respect once given to the past and tradition. The "Prologue" must erase these marks to reduce Venus-Aphrodite to the level of absurd Priapus. Not only Aphrodite and Artemis, Dalhberg asserts, but also the "nereids, nymphs, hamadryads, naiads came out of the sporting houses of elysium," and all Greek worship was "a theology of bawds." And if all classic myth is scorned, Greek history is also reduced, to a record of wisdom degraded by a subservience to mere lust: "Olympia assuaged the rotten fever of Bion, the Philosopher; Theoris served Sophocles in his old age."

In this parody of Greek culture, an accurate picture of any society without either a past or that richness represented by myth, the mind of Priapus is perfectly reflected. His sexuality, which he cannot understand or live with happily without the help of tradition, obsesses him with its urgency, yet the few reminders he still has of the past lead him to confuse his relationship with nature. Governor William Bradford's description of life at Merry Mount demonstrates how deep the Priapic stiffness is set in American history: "They allso set up a Maypole, drinking aboute it many days togeather, inviting the Indian women, for their consorts, dancing and frisking togither, (like so many fairies, or furies rather,) and worse practises. As if they had anew revived and celebrated the feats of the Roman Goddes Flora, or the beasly practieses of the madd Bacchinalians." In his classical allusions, Bradford displays no love for myth, nothing more than contempt for the past; he is absurd in his poorly-disguised obsession with sex; but the ritual described shows how the past in terms of myth can renew the land and gladden the hearts of men. Especially in the "beasly practieses" which would relate man to the animal world, the passage suggests how to separate the narrow morality of the Church from the morality that goes much deeper into the mystery of creation.

Like Gourmont's *Physique de l'amour*, Dahlberg's "Moral Book of Erotic Beasts" is a catalogue of the sexual habits of animals. Unlike Gourmont, Dahlberg attempts to disclaim the relationship of his work to scientific reason: "This is a fable and not natural history." Gourmont belonged spiritually to the Enlightenment, hoping optimistically for the rationality of man to solve the eternal human problems; Dahlberg wisely sees this as a dead end which has led to failure. He therefore offers fable—i.e., myth—instead of natural history. Zoology is morally useless because it is fully rational and man is not. "The mind is as easily thrown down as the senses." And conversely, the rational in man always baffles the animal in him. Neither can Dahlberg share the optimism of Whitman, who made

77

man's ambiguous relationship to the animal word a sign of strength: "I have distanced what is behind me for good reasons,/ But call anything back again when I desire it." Sadly, Dahlberg replies, "In what manner is Messalina superior to the puma?" and demonstrates the absurdity of intellectual primitivism. "The learned, crouched over their inkpots, covet the customs of the savage who cohabits with a Lais or Aspasia of the Amazons whenever he pleases, or envy the panther." Myth, which is not primitive but primordial, unites man with nature at a deeper level by going into the imagination and tracing man's origins beyond the savage and the animal to the point where "man was mist and sea water." In its movement from man to mammals, to birds, to plants and finally to myths of creation, "The Moral Book of Erotic Beasts" is of course much more than a bestiary: its scope is encyclopedic and its retrospective movement embraces the entire history of living matter.

The ancient associations of Priapus with nature as a garden suggest that his plight is tragic mainly in his own eyes. In the garden like Adam and like all citizens of the New World, he is free to perform the rite of naming the beasts and to recreate his world through this ritual. But Priapus lives intellectually in a desert which his mind has created for him, a world described in *The Flea of Sodom* as the fruit of the Rational Tree. Because "the Tree of Reason yields Babel and Sodom and Gomorrah" the figure of Priapus is bestial rather than god-like, no ruler of the beasts. An inhabitant of both desert and garden, Priapus is not truly tragic, but ironically absurd.

The absurdity of such a situation amuses Dahlberg: "A man may want to study Mark, or Paracelsus, or go on an errand to do a kindness to an aged woman, but this tyrant [Priapus the phallus] wants to discharge itself either because the etesian gales are acerb or a wench has just stooped over to gather her laundry. The whole matter, when one thinks of it reasonably, is bizarre." Gourmont had seen the bizarre in such zoological accounts as that of two amorous vultures: "The female, shut in the carcass of an almost devoured horse, interrupted her pecking of carrion to groan deeply, turning her head to look up into the air. A male vulture soared above the larder, replying to the groans of the female. . . . [After considerable sexual play] the union finally took place in a great commotion of

78

ruffled feathers and shaken bones." Dahlberg's irony—though similar—goes much deeper than this because it is part of his style, per-
meating every sentence in ironic vocabulary or syntax. "Man is
double," he says, and the doubleness of his irony continually reminds us of this fact.

In a manner reminiscent of Thoreau, Dahlberg achieves some of
his ironic effects by shifting suddenly from one kind of diction to
another: "Man hates what he does, and that is what is moral in
him, but he continues to do it, which is why he is Euripides, a spi-
der, or the *Dryophis fulgida*." At the end of this series, scientific
Latin is so unexpected that the surprise can be used to ridicule our
best efforts to understand the insects rationally, at the same time
that it ridicules the poet's desires to be like the animals. Similarly,
scientific terminology undercuts the preceding parts of a sentence
to parallel the destruction of myth by rationalism: "Helen, born of
Leda, and the swan, is the most adept voluptuary of the palmated
birds." Although *palmated* literally means "webbed," the sentence
also suggests that it could mean "having palms or hands." This
double meaning reflects the animal-human doubleness of Helen
which is the unstated import of the sentence.

Dahlberg's irony is often fashioned entirely by syntax, but in
this, too, the double is apparent: "Ham and his son Cush were the
original artists, for painting is all about the nudity of other people
and ourselves." *And ourselves*, suddenly doubling the groups involved, makes the concern with others' nakedness turn back ironically and reveal us naked. Sometimes syntactic doubling appears as
parallel clauses: "Euripides was a misogynist, but Sophocles said
that though he hated women in his Tragedies, he found them rap-
turous creatures in his bed." Other times, the double nature of man
appears in a sentence's simply connected clauses: "Men are con-
sumed by their intellects, and what pard, jaguar, or ospry could
bear to be so despoiled."

But more central than the ironic dimensions to Dahlberg's style
are his apothegmatic devices. Objectively, the apothegm is a short
pithy statement resembling the proverb and the epigram. Conventionally, it is related to classical terseness (especially to the economy of the epigram); to religious truth (especially to the Biblical

wisdom of Solomon's Proverbs); and to the wise saws of farmers and others close to the soil (especially to the sharp sayings of old Yankee whittlers). All of these operate to link the style of Dahlberg's bestiary with the wisdom of the past and to a literary form which is seldom associated with original or new ideas. In Gourmont's *Physique de l'amour*, apothegmatic sentences appear, it is true: "Coupling is nearly always a grimace"; "the penis is a luxury and a danger: the bird who does without it is no less wanton thereby"; "Man ought to have the penial bone; he has lost it in the course of ages, and this is doubtless fortunate, for a permanent rigidity, or one too easily obtained, would have increased, perhaps to madness, the salacity of the species." Even if the last of these were more concise, the distinction between these witty epigrams and those of Dahlberg is certainly that they are not intended to express formally the writer's attitude toward ancient wisdom and that they do not set the tone of the entire book. Every paragraph of Dahlberg's "Moral Book" is made up of apothegms and sentences which resemble them closely in length and syntax.

A short, typical paragraph illustrates the dominance and ubiquity of the apothegm:

> Who can dare give his heart to another without panting with fear; for his trust bleats in his bones. The albatross sports with the frigate, the dolphin, and the shark without filling the stomach of one of his companions, and this is a proverb. He is a corpulent rover of the seas, but his belly, when opened, contains nothing but mucilage, and is the envy of Seneca.

The first sentence of this paragraph follows the common syntactic pattern of the book of Proverbs by its separation into two parts and a less common rhetorical pattern in the question, but both patterns are unmistakably Biblical (Proverbs 17:16—"Why should a fool have a price in his hand to buy wisdom, when he has no mind.") In adding, "and this is a proverb" to the next apothegm, Dahlberg seems to suggest that since the information is proverbial, common knowledge, it has special claim to our attention. And because most of what he says is in one sense or another a proverb, the effect of the statement is to ironically reverse itself: the information about the albatross is merely "what people say," though it may contain a mythical truth. The last sentence repeats the Proverbs pattern of the parallel clauses joined by *but*, while the allusion to Seneca's asceticism again adds a note of irony to the wisdom: even Seneca the philosopher cannot conquer his appetites as the albatross has done.

Although more concise apothegms occasionally appear ("A strong foe is better than a weak friend"; "Honeycomb is exile; hellebore is home") the examples already cited give an accurate view of how pervasive is the tone of traditional wisdom. The most significant effect of the apothegmatic style, however, is its discontinuity. Each sentence stands alone. The lack of connection by pronouns is significant. The paragraph is a collection of separate sentences, not a logically related unit. This discontinuity not only demands of the reader an unusual capacity for seeing unity where it is not apparent ("a book for brave readers and poets," Dahlberg calls *The Sorrows*), but it also turns the reader back to a time almost lost in the mists of literary history when the bestiary was a primordial list, a creative ritual, and very close to myth.

Moving back through the age of science while making ironic references to its moral emptiness, Dahlberg arrives at the origin of the bestiary. The radical discontinuity of his style emphasizes how far back he has gone and how many of the associations of the genre with science he has rejected. Only in myth may the need of man to know his place in creation be satisfied, so in myth the creative power of the poet replaces the analytic power of the scientist. In *The Flea of Sodom* Dahlberg had asked, "What advantage has it been to human understanding for man to fawn upon the atom of Democritus of Abdera, and to scorn Hesiod's myth of creation, the Attic lore so similar to Adam's progeny of stones and demons?" "The Moral Book of Erotic Beasts" is the answer, and "The Myth Gatherers," which is the second part of *The Sorrows*, therefore offers Americans a body of myths which can take the place of a morally useless natural history.

Dahlberg's love of American myth is a quality he shares with the greatest American writers, but he is most notably like Thoreau in this book. Our twentieth-century Thoreau, seeking the understanding of the past which will be the understanding of our land and our-

81

selves, says substantially what Thoreau might say if he were writing today; but he does not imitate Thoreau—or anyone else—in any derivative way. Dahlberg knows the value of literary convention and traditional morality, yet his work is unquestionably creative and new. His career demonstrates that there is no tradition for American writers. "We are the eternal infant aboriginals," as he has said, and each artist must take the journey into the backwoods alone if he is to reach the plateau of achievement where Edward Dahlberg now stands.

ALLEN TATE

A GREAT STYLIST: THE PROPHET AS CRITIC

MR. EDWARD DAHLBERG's *Can These Bones Live* is an American classic, even if only a few people know it; but what kind of classic, it is difficult to say. Criticism as we write it at present has no place for it, and this means that I shall probably not be able to do justice to my own admiration. Mr. Dahlberg, like Thoreau whom he admires more than any other nineteenth-century American, eludes his contemporaries; he may have to wait for understanding until the historians of ideas of the next generation can place him historically. For we have at present neither literary nor historical standards which can guide us into Mr. Dahlberg's books written since *Bottom Dogs*, which was published more than thirty years ago. It is significant that he has repudiated this early, naturalistic novel, in spite of the considerable admiration that it won and still retains among a few persons. *Can These Bones Live* may be seen as the summation of a three-part visionary and prophetic work which includes *The Flea of Sodom* and *The Sorrows of Priapus*.

We shall get nowhere with Mr. Dahlberg if we begin with an enquiry into his influences and his philosophy; this kind of thinking would inevitably be reductive. We must return repeatedly to the text to ponder hundreds of aphorisms, epigrams, and paradoxes which add up to an intuitive synthesis of insights which defies logical exposition. The immediate tradition in which Mr. Dahlberg finds himself (*he* did not find *it* or deliberately construct it) is American, and it has a span of more than a century: his mind plays

83

back and forth between Henry David Thoreau and Randolph Bourne, but that the vision has this American stance is only the accident of Mr. Dahlberg's being an American; for the range of allusion and insight is universal and unhistorical and would probably be what it is had the author been born in Rumania and never left there.

It could be said that Mr. Dahlberg is anti-historical, history being the temporal account of man as he exists in and for the state. Mr. Dahlberg, in the line of Thoreau and Bourne, rejects the state:

> Doctrinaire guides, Martin Luther, Marx, Lenin, have been State idealists, the great man-eaters in history. Lenin promised that the State would wither away, but nay, it is not the State but the people that wither away.
>
> All dogmas lead men to the abyss; doctrine is the enemy of vision and the denial of the past. This is what Bourne meant by the "new orthodoxies of propaganda." The ideologue sets up the history of mankind so that his acts can be State-chronicled from the year One. Rifle man of the reminiscences of the race and you enslave him. Without memory man is a most rueful and stumbling creature, coerced to dwell in the dungy cave of the Cyclops.

Although the enormous vitality of the style has sources in Hebraic and Classical cultures, this book is a brilliant and profound survey of American literature. In the passage just quoted, the allusion to the Cave of the Cyclops is no mere literary embellishment; it relates the vision of the present to the experience of the past, and fills the space between, in a timeless intuition of supra-historical man. I do not know any formal critic whose "method" would allow him the sudden collocations and analogies which Mr. Dahlberg can call upon at will to extend and deepen his insights.

I should like to illustrate at some length Mr. Dahlberg's gift for comparative insight which permits him to see American writers against the background of the past. Here he is talking about Whitman and Poe, and when he is done he reaches casually into the past, putting his finger upon Dante, and *illustrates* with great precision (there is no *definition*) the limitations of the Americans.

84

With a deep and reassuring remembrance of the poets who had gone before him, Whitman might have made *Leaves of Grass* an Homeric utterance instead of a revivalistic chant of sex that too often recalls the rank and gaudy age that produced Henry Ward Beecher and Mary Baker Eddy. . . . Europeans compose testaments, journals, poems, but we have to make a Genesis, a Democratic Hygiene. . . .

Take that other aboriginal of diabolism, Edgar Poe. He, like Whitman, had almost no past. Walt Whitman was the pioneer Cosmos, before him nothing. He was innocent, arm-pitted Man before the great Pollution, the Fall, and Edgar Poe was the brand-new Adamic Evil, the original serpent in the Garden. Poe had to invent everything because he remembered almost nothing. . . . A *rathskeller* Vulcan, Edgar Poe hammered out upon the smithy of his moaning soul little Gothic Petroushkas, mechanical horror dolls, Ligeia, Una and Monos.

There are two more paragraphs about Poe; then this summary of the argument by means of illustration:

The fetish of originality is our curse. Dante took a guide. What a myth of Memory is the journey through the *Inferno* where the Poet sees, talks to and weeps with each smitten and hapless ghost.

This looks like a rejection of Poe and Whitman, but it is rather the awareness of an historical perspective. Later on in the book, in the chapter called "Woman," Poe is given extensive treatment which concludes not with a "critical" evaluation but with a visionary allusion:

Of a seemly brow and of an august temperament, he was anointed a Monarch-Poet, but a malignant Star was upon him. Like anguished King Saul, who lost Israel when he tore the skirts of the Prophet Samuel, Poe's genius was a forfeited Kingdom.

In the last chapter Mr. Dahlberg returns to the relation of man to the state. He says: "Each generation must drink deeply its own tragic life." His tragic vision of the human condition redeems what

85

might otherwise appear to be a kind of romantic anarchism, a total rejection of man *in* society, or of men *as* society.

He does not know what kind of society men should have; but he knows what the complete man should be; and he knows that the complete man cannot develop under the State. Where did Dante find his guide? Mr. Dahlberg's brief passage, that I have quoted on this subject, might suggest a focus of the historical imagination that the prophetic vision overlooks. Dante's guide was not just "another poet" who had lived in the past, thus providing a merely literary tradition; Vergil represented the utmost reach of the secular imagination as reason; and this rational, secular imagination had, for Dante, found its limit in the idea of Rome, or the City, which was to be transcended but not abolished by the superaddition of the City of God. This City was not the State as we know it, and there was no provision in it for the idea of Civil Disobedience which Mr. Dahlberg opposes to the Statism of our time. Does he see all societies as forms of Statism? I suspect that he does; and to the extent that he does he tends to see the poet as the perpetual dissenter and outcast. Dante was exiled from his City, with a price on his head; but what had brought this upon him he accepted in principle since he could not have entertained a theory which would justify resistance *as such* to the City. But these considerations apart, we must be grateful to Mr. Dahlberg for allowing this book to be republished, for as Sir Herbert Read says in his Preface, "It is this all-pervasive human wisdom which draws one to the book again and again." When it was first published, more than twenty years ago, the late Ford Madox Ford called it a "work of genius," an opinion with which I whole-heartedly agree. In conclusion I shall cite two passages which further illustrate the versatility and depth of Mr. Dahlberg's insights. The first is an example of the particular literary perception:

> Whitman's Mass "I" is the cold algebraical multitude, and his "evangel-poem of love and comrades" is a Quaker abstract Adam and Eve. There is not one individual woman, name, face or dress; no Bathsheba's hair to catch a David; no Abigail, or Homeric handmaidens.

ALLEN TATE

Here is the relation of Whitman's Mass "I" to its society:

The "awakened" worker is the soviet Osirian corn-maker and god of May Day, crops, socialized cattle and agriculture, who himself *requires* a leader, a communist shaman who has sole power over the mystical collective hands, eyes and genital organs of the Workers' Fatherland. The mystical identity between the state and the proletariat always makes the latter the sacrificial flesh and blood of the former.

I submit that one may learn more about the human condition in our time from this book than from a dozen labored sociological tracts.

Victor Lipton

"CUDGELS AND DISTAFFS, FOR THE REBIRTH . . ."

Can These Bones Live, now somewhat revised, originally appeared in 1941 with a red and black jacket that was more apposite, really, to its content—for under this guise it resembled one of those Marxist texts of the Thirties with revolutionary import. It was indeed a "subversive" work—but its subversion, in this instance, went far beyond the Marxist scope. A "dog beneath the skin" struck out at the presumptions of a Marxist age, as it still does. The implications of the work, with its attack upon the basic rationalism of our age, reach far beyond the conventional anti-communism and anti-Marxist criticism that began to appear about the time of Dahlberg's work. Thus, while the sun of anti-Marxist criticism may be setting, Dahlberg's work remains apart, both by its content and by the vitality and freshness of its prose. *Can These Bones Live* deserves an attention that has so far been withheld from it by all but a percipient few.

Perhaps the somewhat strident tone of the author has blurred the essential value of this work. Anyone who presumes to challenge such writers as Melville, Thoreau, Poe and Whitman may be looked upon with suspicion by the academic orthodoxy, though Dahlberg often acknowledges their genius and has only unalloyed admiration to offer Cervantes, Shakespeare and Dostoyevsky. Not since D. H. Lawrence's *Studies in Classic American Literature* have we had such a provocative study, one which is similar in theme and yet goes beyond it in its more basic attack, which returns us to an archaic polytheism.

89

There is one curious contradiction in this fascinating study of our tradition. While chastising our writers for an alleged personal inhibition that limits their effectiveness as artists, Dahlberg also comes to grips with a point that is often lost by critics as well as admirers of our culture. He states, especially in his essay on Thoreau, that the rationalistic and inhibitory civilization of the West cannot be equated with its men of culture. The latter geniuses are "accidents in time" whose merit is their essential negation of the civilization which nurtured them. Thus Dahlberg answers the idolization of such aforementioned writers as "products" of civilization—this dubious "praise," in his eyes, virtually negates them as forces for our time, and hastens them into limbo.

It may be that in order to resurrect them today as living entities for our age he has had to criticize them in an unduly harsh manner in order to get rid of this false idolatry. The moot question is not whether he has thrown out the baby with the bath but whether he has confused the two. It may be that we must expect a certain limited functioning as people in our writers, who, if they were more fortunate in their personal lives, might be driven altogether crazy by the social contradictions which their writing opposed.

Nonetheless, the observations by this very sensitive critic are always of value even when his criticisms, like Lawrence's, sometimes ideologize art out of all existence. But Dahlberg digs deeper into a criticism of "the life" than do most esthetic critics, and by doing so he has something more important than the "esthetic" to say about present-day society. In relation to Lawrence's work, Dahlberg's reflects a greater despair, and indirectly speaks to the heart of all the contemporary rationale or ideology, the ideology of unlimited progress and industrialization. This is more likely to bring about the kind of change to the classical values that Dahlberg espouses.

Dahlberg starts with the conflict of the poet against the state, such as that in Thoreau and Randolph Bourne. The fact that officialdom, today, praises someone like Thoreau and anthologizes him is hypocritical behavior but also shows cunning. It makes this writer whose "thoughts were murder to the state" into a classic and so milks him of significance. Dahlberg's respect for Thoreau is deep but not altogether uncritical. On the one hand he is the epitome of

VICTOR LIPTON

all artists who must always be outside the state itself. He is, in our contemporary Wilsonian—that is, *Colin* Wilsonian phrase—the "outsider." One might remember the basic Marxist literary doctrine (held by many schools of literary criticism) of the Thirties, when this book of Dahlberg's was written, was that the artist reflects his time and sums up its social aspirations. In the section entitled "The Helmet of Mambrino," Dahlberg contrasts "behavioristic" writers with those "true realists" who "always cause us to exclaim, 'I never saw a room, a table, a cloud, a woman, act like that before!' " The true artist opposes ordinary reality, ideology, and the state.

On the other hand, and this attitude is rather recurrent throughout this work, Dahlberg criticizes Thoreau for certain evidences that he was himself an inhibited artist who did not act as freely and naturally as he might (or as Dahlberg wished him to). Thoreau could never "stop loathing his low mortal habits," Dahlberg complains. Thoreau did see a value in the ordinary man of the village, however, and wished he could be like him. Dahlberg shows little sympathy with the artist as a person, and the relation he makes between his personal habits and his writing is often a too direct one. The criticism that results is more despairing and untrue than justice would allow or taste would pass, even though this desperation may be symbolically relevant to today's situation.

But he comments on Bourne's personal deformity with some approval. He is like the Fool in *Lear*, or Thersites, and represents the ugliness of truth to some. Bourne represents to Dahlberg a kind of poetic and personal rejection of the state power, the individual who arises on the scene to prove that "the parts are greater than the whole." Both Dahlberg and Bourne, like Toynbee, reject the Spenglerian (and Platonic and Marxian) notion of the state as a grandiose "biological" organism to which one owes primary allegiance over one's own. Bourne, in his quasi-deformed flesh, represents to Dahlberg the existential rejection of this notion. In considering Bourne's "impossibilism," Dahlberg sees two distinct currents in human history existing at the same time "chronologically," but like Proust, in different personal times. History and art are irreconcilable. Personal time is concerned with Dostoyevsky, Shakespeare, etc., like Malraux's "museum without walls." One doesn't need dog-

91

mas or creeds to inform one of the evil of war, disease, poverty, to comprehend Proudhon's "property is theft." The objection to the state should be instinctual, and Dahlberg sees or seeks an affinity with Bourne who rejected the radicalism of his day, as he, Dahlberg, did of the Thirties, and went instead to personal objection.

It is only the selection of the texts that one wonders about; how "instinctual" for his own good man really is. Dahlberg at times criticizes, like an old radical, the environment for leading men astray, at others, man's own propensity to be fooled. One suspects that often the modern texts—like Proudhon's—are capriciously rejected out of hand, but the classical texts "always" help man with his instincts!

In the section entitled "Ishmael," Dahlberg explores the reasons for the antagonism of America towards its artists. It curiously tends to become an attack upon these artists themselves! Yet there are some telling points. He finds them trapped, lonely giants who mostly had to lift themselves by their own bootstraps, to chart new ways. Somewhat contradicting the points made in his studies on Thoreau and Bourne, he feels they could have profited by having a tradition to study, and other men of letters around with whom to converse. They are lonely Ishmaels, "doomed to be cut away, afar from earthly mortal beginnings, the human vineyards, the beauteous Genesis of the protean and warming race-experience." Yet, instead of seeing this as a tragic condition of the Western artist, Dahlberg levies his attack here more upon the artists than upon the age or its inhibitory ideology. One might interpret these pages as self-revelatory, in fact, as such a remark that "the four or five beauteous spirits of our nineteenth century were only dimly aware of one another's existence . . ."! And when Dahlberg shows how this exclusion and separation hindered their development as artists and human beings, one wonders, as one cannot blame one individual writer more than another among these contemporaries, whether they can be blamed together, or who or what to blame?

In "Sanctified Lies," Dahlberg attacks our critics for their over-sanctification of genius after he is dead (and this present, more "invidious" Dahlbergian treatment of our writers seems to have been done out of tremendous implicit respect for them!). With Shavian abruptness, Dahlberg strikes out, "We have not lacked poets, but

92

what we have most mournfully missed are critics." Woodberry, Perry, Parrington and Brownell are "the sterile grammarians of American Literature," who have created the "lie" of an American renaissance around our great lonely writers, by dragging up such as Dunlap, Freneau and Brown (who were they, indeed?). Dahlberg often wonderfully hits issues just right. For the Whitman pietists, the *Leaves of Grass* was as a "laying on of hands"! Then Dahlberg excoriates those modern critics—Croce, Kant, Bosanquet, I. A. Richards—who continue "the critical humbug, disguised as scientific or esthetic or proletarian analyses of literature," all those who try to reduce the tragic element in our artists to a recognizable formula. He attacks, in a telling phrase, the "marxian Poloniuses of class-conscious literature." He sees the critic as "the Sancho Panza to his master, our Lord Don Quixote, the artist."

In this section on criticism, Dahlberg echoes the artist's own suspicion of the critic as the representative of that orthodoxy his—the artist's—whole function must oppose.

The antagonism of America to the artist lies, perhaps, as much in her critics, Dahlberg suggests, as in her Puritanism. Though the early Puritans were, in fact (he thinks), more sensual and closer to the earth, they did not deny "fleshly man," and the reason for this antagonism cannot be found here.

Early America was a kind of new Eden which Dahlberg finds to approximate closely the Hesiodic "Works and Days" existence of classical times. It is all the more exasperating to him to see this promise develop as it did. "Almost the whole of American Literature has been a deep refusal of man," he laments in "The Flesh Refused." "America for a hundred years was a vineyard," says Dahlberg, who loves the grape and the land, in other words, Eden. Our writers are, he thinks, though powerful contradictions of our modern malaise, also "dry bones" themselves.

The "sensual Puritan" lived close to the soil, "to the fields, the house, reverentially white, the orchard." The former derived "from Abraham, Noah and Job . . . the ecstasy and fervor he had for his sheep, apples, wood, grain." Pointing to the parallel classical certainties (about life itself), Dahlberg finds the "colonial farm house, rooted in, and winging upwards from, the soil, bespeaks the miracles of growth, life, birth, procreation, marriage." And again,

93

placing recent myth against old myth, he says that "the Puritan's churchly slaying of the sexual organs, like the dismemberment of Osiris, was a furtive and diabolical worship of seedtime, spring, copulation." Dahlberg interestingly points to the abstract and cold qualities of Marsden Hartley's seascapes ("dead birch logs, stones"); nor do the "bloodless wash of sedge, marge, bay" of John Marin's water colors fare better. And he puns on the watery-ness of American painting! With abstraction in painting, literature or life Dahlberg will have nothing to do. Dahlberg comes close, in these pages, to attacking, as in recent years the philosopher Jack Jones has attacked outright and more directly, rationalism itself as the focal point of our ideology and the ultimate cause of this abstraction in art and life.

Returning to our literature, Dahlberg deplores the fact that "in almost a hundred years of American Literature we do not have one feeding, breeding, sexual male, not one aching, suffering, bedpining Manon Lescaut, Daudet's Sappho or Madame Bovary. There are no ripe women here." Unlike Chekhov and Dostoyevsky, whose feelings are evident in their works, our writers cloak their feelings in hieroglyphics which need deciphering. And "refusals beget deeper refusals," he states. The American experiment, he concludes sadly, is a kind of cosmic intrusion into history which has failed:

Here is the whole allegory of the Fall of Man in the American Garden of Eden. After Hester Prynne, after Ligeia, Eleonora, there is nothing left but the Iron Phallus, [Henry] Adams' nine foot pistons.

Dahlberg's own profession of faith indicates the direction criticism too must take if it is to understand and approximate the artist:

There are no abstract truths,—no Mass-Man, no proletariat. There is only Man. When the Pulse has been nailed upon the crossbeams, lo, Reason gives up its viable breath and becomes a wandering ghostly Error. Truth and folly are ever about to expire, so that we like our beloved Sancho Panza, kneeling at the death-bed of Don Quixote, must always be ready to go out to receive the holy communion of cudgels and distaffs, for the rebirth of the Pulse.

94

Josephine Herbst

EDWARD DAHLBERG'S *BECAUSE I WAS FLESH*

Edward Dahlberg calls *Because I Was Flesh* an autobiography. And so it is. But it is autobiography of a peculiar kind. Dahlberg's development, from the completion of his first novel, *Bottom Dogs,* in 1928, to the present day, has been both rich and graveled, complicated and various. It is easy to describe second rate talents; they fall into a class and enlist under a standard. But first rate powers defy comparison and can be defined only by themselves.

Dahlberg has rejected his early novels and has called them "mistakes" and perhaps they should be regarded only as the prehistory of his serious accomplishments. But there are intersecting veins of life between the early and the later work, there is an insistent pulse of feeling which required *Because I Was Flesh* for full revelation. For this insistent pulse relates to his mother, and this is a memoir of her life on earth and the unraveling of her fate which Dahlberg identifies with his own. In the light of *Because I Was Flesh* one can say that all of Dahlberg's search has been for the few great images which gained real access to his heart. They interpret, as nothing else can ever do, all the rest. The rigors of the period, its agonizing shocks and dislocations, decimated more writers than death itself. It is no less than phenomenal that Dahlberg continuously survived as a creative artist, and, suffering his own mutations, has given us a masterpiece.

Because I Was Flesh assumed all the years of Dahlberg's life in the making. It began in a charity hospital in Boston when his mother gave him her father's name "to hide the fact that I was as illegitimate as the pismire, the moth or the prince." Note the language. In this book every word has a voice. He chooses "pismire," rejecting the less vocative "ant." In three words he is sorting out the tea-leaf prophecies of his fortune; he will *be* the pismire, as surely as the fitful, wayward moth or the proud prince. He will be both abased and exalted. Insulted and injured, he will refuse to rot. He dedicated his studies of classic American and world literature, *Can These Bones Live*, to the memory of his mother, who, "as a sorrowing Hagar, taught me to make Ishmael's Covenant with the Heart's Afflictions." But if he is an Ishmael, he is also one who wrestles for the light with the demons of darkness, calling upon his angels.

There *are* angels, as surely as there are demons. Who cannot recognize the one will refuse the other. To live without angels is to dwell in limbo. Rude daily life may hide the angel in anonymity; death can stir the murmuring wings. For his mother and her Star Ladies Barber Shop to become a mythic source of insight and strength for Dahlberg there had to be a long detour into a past more remote than his own boyhood.

Sometime after 1936, he must have cleared a space for himself, however brief, of a deliberate absence from the obligations and expectations of the active world he aimed to master by retreat, in which the most delicate elements of life are refreshed and comforted, while the inner creature is in some way cleansed of its stains. Such a moment is more than detachment, for it requires more than separation from the rowdy day. It requires a stillness in which the voices of the oracles may be heard. For once Dahlberg had changed over from the world of his first three novels, he was listening for the oracles, and awaiting the gods. And he was appointing himself the architect of his own Kosmos in which no surprises or alien pressures could betray him to self-treachery.

You might say that contempt for the present, hatred for the living generation, and self-loathing led him to take the path to primordial sources, did he not indicate, with utter clarity, that the miracle of perception is involved with the miracle of love. Or, that, in *The Sorrows of Priapus*, when he takes Greek natural philosophers, Hebrew prophets, Hakluyt, Monardes and de Vaca as guides to roam through five millennia of mythological lore, it might be that he is searching only for Moly, the fabulous herb with the milk white flower and a black root, which Homer said was given by Hermes to Odysseus, to guard against the spells of Circe. The swan, and the Antarctic petrel, the woodland laurel and the squash flower, early societies where work, penance, art and festival were mingled take transcendence, in Dahlberg's fables and gnomic utterances, over Man, as in Pliny, one of his spiritual forebears, who marveling for seven volumes over the wonders of the natural world, commented drily, "The manners of men have degenerated," and, finally getting around to Man, exposes the creature's predicament in a powerful, eloquent and gloomy picture which seems to reflect the colors of the poet Lucretius and to provide subject matter for the meditations of Pascal.

If there is nothing new in Dahlberg's pessimistic view of man, there is nothing new, either, in his preoccupation with a lost Eden. The vision of a lost paradise has been the flickering light for more than one artist from time immemorial, as it has been for the lowly, but especially since the ascent of science has imposed on man the conviction that he is master over the mysterious forces of the universe and the conqueror of Nature, while he forgets, in his conceit, that he is but a tiny drop of Nature, too. Nor need one look only to the modern movement for the voices seeking the magic word to break the crust of the cerebralized self to let the spontaneous, the warm, the mythic light come through. Long before Germany swarmed with "men of brass around whom objects surge" Goethe turned away from the petty dark of a provincial court to the southern sun for its regenerative, creative source. Van Gogh fled for his salvation from the povertied gloom of Belgium and a bigoted father to the almond and olive orchards of light in Provence. "Dark" is no more than a metaphor for an oppressive weight on the flesh and spirit, and it is not surprising that the German Expressionists, in particular, betrayed the greatest need for a regenerative, sensuous paradise. The crushing weight of the German educational system, against which Nietzsche uttered so eloquent a warning, the tyrannical role of the father in the family, the deadly rise of the Philistine, the fatality of the military system, plus the peculiar

97

marginal role of the artist in Germany, could bring a poet like Gottfried Benn to proclaim:

> O that we might be our ancestors' ancestors.
> A little ball of slime in a tepid moor.

And propel the Billionaire in Kaiser's drama, *The Coral*, to exalt the coral, the symbol of the primitive, vegetative life, over the cross, the symbol of the spirit. "Paradise lies behind us," says Kaiser's Billionaire, "and the only way to happiness is the way of retrogression."

But Dahlberg was not looking for "happiness" but for meaning and value. Though he, too, was searching for ancestors, he did not expect to find them in a ball of slime but among the exalted prophets. If we compare his closing lines in *The Sorrows of Priapus* with Gottfried Benn's retrogressive symbols, we can see at once the conclusive difference. Dahlberg writes, "Where are the little hills which shall bring justice, or the fruits of Lebanon? O forest spectre, ferns, lichens, boleti contain Eden. Be primordial or decay." One word does it. The word is *justice*. Justice is not native to the primordial world but belongs to the human. Man may seek justice in vain, but the expectation is one of his nobler attributes.

Dahlberg was not retreating to a fanciful rosy delirium nor looking for something he had lost when he made the long march into the past of the human and animal worlds to rescue the vegetative myths, the rituals and the lore which sprang from a conjunction of the two. If he was submitting himself to a discipline timed to the pulse of his life, could he know where it might lead? As a tutelary muse, Dahlberg was also tutoring himself. You might say he had given himself to the task of reconciling fanaticism with serenity. Taken alone, each is disastrous, yet except through the integration of these two opposites, there is no true art. For nothing can be accomplished without fanaticism, and without serenity, nothing can be perceived in its own identity. Though he states that it is his earnest conviction that "we cannot produce a sublime literature without ritual and legends . . . English must be put back into the ground to grow again," it takes more than noble language to open the tombs.

The right words are important, not any words will ever do. But even if the key turns in the heavy door, there must be something behind its massiveness, worth opening for. That there *was* something was obsessive knowledge, the subject of eternal turnings-over in his mind, musings, revulsions, praise. And though Dahlberg may imagine that his discontent with his early work rests primarily on what he came to feel was the limitation of its style, its neologisms, its too ready reliance on the vernacular, the fact is, that he must also have felt the lesser weight of the experience he had sought to reveal, in contrast with the density of its actuality. For his first three novels could not release him from the bondage of his own life from which he could only be freed by a fanatic persistence to see who he was, within, as he had evolved from circumstances, without. It is the unraveling of this persistent search which makes *Because I Was Flesh* so moving a book, in which its author attains to a mastery over experience by facing its utmost implications.

The minimal background material of *Bottom Dogs* and *Because I Was Flesh* is the same. In each there is the lady barber and her son, and the central locality is Kansas City. In both versions, the lady barber has suffered the same vicissitudes of flight from and pursuit by the barber, with whom she ran away from her husband, a fur operator in Brooklyn, to begin her wanderings in Dallas, Denver, Memphis, finally to land in Kansas City with a barber shop of her own. With her, always, is her son, who is sent at the age of eleven to an orphanage in Cleveland when the river captain, with whom she has taken up, objects to his hanging around. After seven years in the orphanage, the boy returns, and though his mother has been deserted by the captain, he decides to go on the bum. With his vagabondage we need not for the moment be concerned.

D. H. Lawrence, who wrote an introduction for *Bottom Dogs* after the manuscript was sent to him by Arabella York, the second wife of Richard Aldington, expressed shock at Dahlberg's unmasking of the life of the boys in the orphanage: "They are cold wills functioning with a minimum of consciousness. The amount they are *not* aware of is perhaps the most amazing aspect of their character. They are brutally and deliberately unaware. They have no

hopes, no desires even. They have even no will-to-exist, for existence even is too high a term. They have a strange, stony will-to-
persist, that is all. And they persist by reaction, because they still
feel the repulsiveness of each other, of everything, even of themselves. . . . It is, in psychic disintegration, a good many stages ahead
of *Point Counter Point.* . . ."

In a recent issue of the *Texas Quarterly*, Jonathan Williams discusses Dahlberg's writings up to but not including *Because I Was
Flesh*, and comments on D. H. Lawrence's reactions: "Which just
isn't so. As a matter of fact *Bottom Dogs* strikes me as much closer
to *Huckleberry Finn* than to the *Blackboard Jungle* or *Rebel without a Cause*. The cool generation would have given Lawrence a real
crise de fois." He then quotes a section showing the orphans divert-
ing themselves: "They would blow themselves to a pint of ice-
cream, scoop it out with pieces of pasteboard from the box, and sing
on the front porch in their b.v.d.'s: 'The bells are ringing for me
and my gal.' That would get Max into a chatty vein and he would
ramble along like a 1916 Ford. Was Werner, the gardener, really
the kaiser's bodyguard, and how many more weeks would Werner's
nag last? Max said he had once tried to ride him, but that old dob-
bin was harder than Doc's nails, and that he almost split in two."
But the section Williams quotes does not give the texture prevailing in the account of the orphanage in *Bottom Dogs*, which *is* of a
gritty substance, though no orphan commits a murder or runs
hogwild, in latter day style. No playful shenanigans of the orphans
can conceal their identity as waifs or their relationship to the orphanage and to the indifferent world. "The asylum grounds, its
cinders, its junky buildings, the verboten grass and muted water
fountain out front, were in their ruined roots," Dahlberg says
plainly in *Because I Was Flesh*.

And, there seems to me, nothing of Huck Finn in either version
of the orphans, for Huck was a product of an earlier, footloose,
jocund mid-America, where the Mississippi could be his river-god,
and an escaped slave his unforeseen angel. If the entire emphasis
has shifted from the antipathies and revulsions of *Bottom Dogs* to
the luminous insight of *Because I Was Flesh*, it is because Dahlberg
himself had changed over, or, as the German Expressionists called

100

it, had made a "break-through." And, the compulsion for a break-through is nowhere more in evidence than in the account of the orphans. Though in *Bottom Dogs*, as elsewhere in everything Dahlberg has written, he stands aloof, as a solitary, as the stranger among his fellows, he is also one of the sufferers, and the acid of the orphans' condition must be the accusing poison before it can be sucked out by the catalyst as an inner tragic value.

The orphanage, whether in *Bottom Dogs* or *Because I Was Flesh*, is the boy's first close-up view of the regimented life, against which, in whatsoever form it may show itself, Dahlberg will oppose a defiant will for the rest of his mortal existence. The regimen of the orphanage was martial. In *Because I Was Flesh* he tells us: "Scipio, who compelled his troops to eat uncooked food standing up, would have been satisfied with these waifs who rose every morning at 5:30 as though making ready for a forced march. The playgrounds in the back resembled Milton's sooty flag of Acheron. . . ." Though thoughts of food were ever present in their infant minds, the craving for affection was a hidden ache. Nor is it only the orphans who are engaged in warfare. Lizzie Dahlberg was engaged in a war for her life and the cold months had come upon her when she changes the course of her son's fate by shipping him off to the orphanage. For her hope of marriage, and all of her vain expectations, are dictated by the visions of a Don Quixote in another idiom, and Dahlberg will have to make the long voyage out of the world before he can reenter, as the inheritor of her desperado gallantry, to see himself as the son of a lady barber who had provided him with the shaving mug which he had to translate into the helmet of Mambrino.

In mood, and in his groping for the roots of a spiritual experience which was to undergo a variety of mutations, Dahlberg was closer to the German Expressionists of the twenties than he was to his own American contemporaries. In *Bottom Dogs* he was even closer to the early nihilistic Brecht who wrote *In the Jungle of Cities* than he was to the American "exiles" who had simmered through a tempestuous period as rebels more conscious of the "revolution of the word" than as subjects of opaque tumults of human experience. His complete willingness in *Because I Was Flesh* to explore his irreso-

101

lutions and despair, as a writer and a man, remind us of the German, Barlach, who at thirty-four confessed that he had not even begun to feel the slightest assurance about his attempts at art, and, "hiding in the darkest corners of coffeehouses, wished to be invisible, worthy of no attention and hardly in need of it." Barlach turned his own corner by way of *Wandlung*, experienced on a trip to Russia, where Rilke's wanderings among the Russian community and the Russian peasants, earlier in the century, had also led him to a decisive spiritual liberation. Like Barlach, Dahlberg must have been infused, whether directly or indirectly, with the Dostoyevskian acceptance of suffering as the gate to salvation, though the Tolstoy, who was the mediator for Rilke, may have strengthened his own assertiveness in the realm of moral values. And, as Rilke's angels in the *Duino Elegies* are perpetually occupied in transforming the world of outward materialism back into inner tragic values, the reality of the objective world in *Because I Was Flesh* is interpreted by older words which have not lost their pith, or by sayings of the wise, and by correspondences which will reveal the lady barber, in all her final tatters, as a woman who walks like a proverb.

Though Dahlberg may have thought to seal up his early life experiences in *Bottom Dogs*, he was to reopen the theme again in *From Flushing to Calvary*, published in 1932, and in which the story of Lizzie and her son, called Lorry as in *Bottom Dogs*, is continued in the grim anonymity of Bensonhurst, Brooklyn. There is a long procession of characters in the book, as the author was to describe in remarks in *Contempo*: "It is no longer the scene so much, as in *Bottom Dogs*, which is the protagonist, as the kick-about figures who pass through it, for they never act but react upon their environment. . . . Lizzie regrets the day she gave up her lady-barber shop, and Lorry wants to and does run away from his mother to return to the orphanage in Cleveland. And only then does he discover that he is in no place and that no place is in him. . . . The inevitability of the dollarless American trapped in a capitalistic society is one of the essential themes of the book. . . ." If the last sentence is a reminder of Brecht's *Mahagonny* which also had its setting in an American town, though an imaginary one, and where the only value was Money, the theme must also have signified for Dahlberg the urgent need for a break-through.

He was not to make it with his next novel, *Those Who Perish*, 1934, and which may be the first American fiction, as Jonathan Williams suggests, to concern itself with Nazism in America. *Those Who Perish* are a group of Jews, directors and workers, connected with the Community House in a New Jersey city. Dahlberg maneuvers the three major characters in a network of persecutions and horrors, and he gives all three, deaths, which verge on the hysterical and melodramatic. He was to convey the agony of the historical moment, and his characters are particularized and given motivation, but none of them take hold of the reader with the conviction of the people in *Because I Was Flesh*, and the self-propagating image grows like a brilliant fungus all over the prose.

This language was to be even more nervously acerbated in a fragment of a novel to be called *Bitch Goddess* which appeared in the magazine *Signature* in 1936. In this fragment of an uncompleted work, the efforts of the young protagonist to be a writer, throttled by a clutter of events and malign circumstances, is related with sardonic humor. His one solace in his dingy flat is the memory of his dead mother's wings of dark hair and her gardenia perfume, and though the image is conventionalized, it connects, by way of reference, to the author's compulsive willingness to pick at the same themes and characters, over and over, which is the mark of a profound but fertile uncertainty. It is the kind of uncertainty which was a precondition for the creativity of Cézanne when he required his wife to sit through an eternity for each portrait, and which was to compel Dahlberg to submit his experiences to revisions and, finally, to a long submersion in the dark, before they could emerge in the perfected meanings of *Because I Was Flesh*.

In *Because I Was Flesh*, Dahlberg interprets the period of his first novels as a sort of captivity in which, "I had resolved to be a writer and to clean out the Augean stables of society, but there is no meat, bread or potatoes for Hercules, the stableboy. After I had written three novels my plight was no better than that of the niata which starves to death when there is nothing on the pampas but a few twigs and reeds. Nor was I any more apt with a good book merely because I was in the world. . . . After poring over the works of sages I had no less spleen, bile or vanity, and I was just as vacant as I had been. . . . The distance between me and my mother had grown. My life was so hopeless that I wrote a book." Where was he to turn, what to do? In the society of his fellows, he felt himself a solitary. If, like some of his fellow writers of the epoch, he had thought to serve justice by exposing the predicament of the human being caught in the toils of economic-political circumstances, this effort could no longer serve his purpose. For at the end of the decade, the cause of Justice had never seemed more forlorn, and the depersonalized authoritarianism of the orphanage had become the prevailing dark ground of the world. If he turned to the past, away from the temporal chaos, and away from his own constricted consciousness, as well, it was an admission that he needed guides for the interpretation of the contemporary and for the understanding of the self. So, he could say, "The fetish of originality is our curse. Dante took a guide!"

He could cast his three books behind him, as Deucalion his stones, and when in 1941, *Can These Bones Live* appeared, the old language had been purified by fire. The voice is the same voice, and, clarified, it continues to speak for the fundamentals dear to Dahlberg as an artist and a man. If it is an attack on the Modern World, in its disintegrations, its blight called "civilization," and on the superstitions out of which Totalitarian man is the grim breed, it is also a tender examination of the quarries where the bones of our chief writers lie—Melville, Poe, Whitman, Thoreau, Emily Dickinson, Sherwood Anderson—and joined to this, is a chapter mulling over the visions of Dostoyevski, Shakespeare, Christ, and Cervantes. This testament, a formidable sematic work, of dense compactness and provocative content, placed Dahlberg as a master of a superb prose style and a critic of the modern drift; certain to win enemies as well as devoted friends.

When he came to write *Flea of Sodom*, published in 1950, he had retreated backward in historical time, and was now in the company of Ovid, Livy, Strabo, Suetonius, Herodotus, Plutarch, the Book of Enoch and the Apocalypse of Baruch. The line is gnomic, as Sir Herbert Read was to say, and if the "similes themselves are definitions of ancient rituals, which are the bucolic physic for men who feed and gender on our macadam meadows" the voice is that of the poet-teacher and the prophet; in turn, persuasive, beguiling, authoritative, scornful. He was to continue his search for the meaning of the mind and body in myth and experience in *The Sorrows of Priapus*, 1957, the first part of which is an urbane, witty encyclopedia of the appetites and customs of the salacious anthropoid *homo sapiens*, while the second part, called "The Myth Gatherers," distills the old elixirs, by which men once lived and guided their destinies.

Dahlberg, too, would bring back these distillations of ancient wisdom from the magic ring of myth to a bewildered world, but, how teach again, what has been taught correctly and incorrectly learned a hundred-thousand times throughout the ages of man's prudent folly? How awaken the sleepers to the fructifying source? The immensity of the task also engenders despair, and this despair may take the form of an aggressiveness of which the author is not even aware. In these works it consists mainly of the repetitious weight of the learned symbols, which have been absorbed by Dahlberg until they are a parcel of the ardent self. But, perhaps, as Thucydides might say, he has "cast his nets too high" for the reader, who, not used to the lofty company he keeps, may feel in the presence of an arrogant master who boxes his stupid ear, even as he offers a consolatory herb.

Or, is bedeviled, modern man capable of accepting wise warnings when his psyche craves the cathartic experience, or, perversely, the purgatory fire? Dahlberg himself steers to his points, sometimes in the midst of paradox, when he says, "There is knowledge before reason and science, a secret wisdom that is prior to logic, the vibrant god-telling Pulse." Though he frequently reminds us of D. H. Lawrence in his iconoclastic intensity and prophetic probings, he differs from Lawrence, in that his emphasis is not on the dark "blood" but on the "pulse," which is sensitive to the imagination—"man's Holy Ghost."

The difficulty in writing about Dahlberg is that he provides his own texts and in such remarkable, aphoristic, shining language, as to baffle the transmitter. The language can seem a solid, many faceted rock, which can split to gush a pure fountain or hold firm to become a judgment seat. It does become a Judgment Seat when Dahlberg, as Grand Inquisitor, takes apart twentieth century authors in *Truth is More Sacred*. In this volume of back-and-forth letters with Sir Herbert Read, Dahlberg would shatter the image of Joyce, Henry James, D. H. Lawrence, Ezra Pound, T. S. Eliot, and Robert Graves, while Sir Herbert demurs, improvises and placates the images again. Dahlberg is himself when he praises or decries; he needs moral pretexts to show his wit and eloquence. But in *Truth is More Sacred* the stern moralist completely prevails over the man of sensibilities; Henry James incites him only to revulsion; Joyce writes a "canting, riff-raff English." Eliot and Pound "bait their readers as if they were angling for mullets: they snare them with a morsel of Dante, a quotation from Marlowe . . . or from St. John of the Cross, or by simply mentioning Agamemnon, Odysseus, Menelaus or Clement of Alexandria . . ." and, in view of Dahlberg's profuse use of learned citations, however otherwise employed, this is an astounding malediction! Sir Herbert reminds Dahlberg: "You are absolute for truth . . . and would send to the stake any author who in any respect offends your dogma. That dogma is not strictly aesthetic . . . on the contrary, you have spoken of virtue and health. Your conception of the great writer is that of a sage or a seer, a patriarch who instructs his people in a voice of authority, and castigates them with whips of scorn when they are weak and errant."

It is astonishing, therefore, to find in *Because I Was Flesh* that Dahlberg has taken the deadweight out of his teaching as a didactic writer, and has launched his basic theme on the confusing, chopping and changing current of individual human life. Though there is solid moral ground and not a sea of shifting relative values, it is absorbed as part of the organic drama. The objective matter of the earlier novels has not been altered except in minor details; fundamentally, it is all here. But the images have been given life, not by an interesting application of references to remote history, but by the illuminations Dahlberg has gained through an experienced distance, and from his journeyings into an inspired past. Thus, Liz-

106

zie's hands, which in *Bottom Dogs* are only capable and sturdy, are now seen in the light of eternity, for they have "the soul of a pentagram, which Plato considered the geometric figure of goodness." We believe those hands because they belong to a mother whose son confesses that her long nose sorely vexed him. "I don't believe I ever forgave her for that, and when her hair grew perilously thin, showing the vulgar henna dye, I thought I was the unluckiest son in the world."

If this is a confessional, it is a redemptive one, in which the author's ego has died down to admit the fallen and guilty son, that he might be reborn to an acceptance of human destiny through suffering and vision. Where another writer might state beliefs, Dahlberg breaks belief down into its shifting phases, as though it were a fate, an unsought suffering that has descended upon us. He catches the very processes of April hope as it first stirs, breaking up the personality to particles, for his people all have the amazing dramatic aptitude for becoming their opposites. The double role in Dahlberg's characters operates simultaneously; pride and abasement, love and hate, cruelty and tenderness do not mingle, but assert themselves, dramatically and incongruously, side by side. The son confesses that though he longed to be a Sardanapalus, nothing came of his aspirations; he was so helpless that he could not even get the pox, and "pined for erudition, a half hour with a prostitute and a magnificent infectious disease."

Though all of these people, and especially Lizzie and her son, live in a maniacal inner solitariness, it is all the more convincing because of the gregariousness of their surroundings. Lizzie operates a flourishing barber shop into which customers stream from seven in the morning until late at night. She trains girls to become barbers, too, and gives them board and room, even concocting herbal potions to bring them around when fooling with a sharp traveling-man gets them in trouble. They are a lusty band of wenches who often appear more suitable for a Madame Tellier's Establishment than for a barber shop, but each of them is also a solitary, though she may support a chick of a child. Lizzie's suitors arrive, one by one, with their hearts on their sleeves, but soon turn out to have a wife already, or a leeching sister in the background, or like Henry Smith, the river captain, move off with a puerile titter to join a worthless chippy. But life is made endurable by sexual love and usage; only these relieve the relentless and unremitting irony of circumstances. So Popkin will marry her to fleece her, and to return to his former wife. Her "cultured matrimonial ad" will be answered by a stingy ancient who will not even remove his overshoes or lay aside an umbrella.

The book is packed with living people, each trailing his or her irrelevant baggage, but how important Dahlberg's obsession with human souls becomes when we see these lives emerge in physical explicitness to insist on being what they actually are! Even his minor figures are distinctive and this suggests fertility of the imagination. The humor by which they make themselves known, is implicit, refined by the comic spirit to admit defeat—nothing to be done!—which, at the same time, asserts victory—never give in.

Lizzie Dahlberg was born of a family living outside Warsaw; among her ancestors there were as many Catholics as Jews. A strong Polish strain shows in Dahlberg's Slavic cheekbones. His spirited mother left home when she was sixteen to escape a bigoted grandmother, and, reaching America, was handed over in marriage to an inept fur operator by an older brother, who could contrive nothing better. When she runs off with Saul, the barber, enticed by his vulpine locks and milk-white teeth, she is leaping from the frying pan into the fire, for he is a licentious woman-chaser, who will rob her and her son for other women when he can. After she learns Saul's trade, a cowpuncher in Dallas would rather have his throat cut by Lizzie than his chin scraped by Saul. The boy witnesses violent scenes, early in life, but as his mother always flees Saul to save him, he is precociously aware of his powerful position as the important male. Though his situation later on is imperiled by his mother's suitors, even shipment to the orphanage does not induce a cynical hardness. If the impulse to look "inside" never freezes, it is because the mythic bond with his mother is firmly set, for all time, and this bond will even become the source of strength which allows him to paint her portrait in *Because I Was Flesh* with the utmost relentlessness, and with the utmost love.

The fact is that in *Because I Was Flesh*, Dahlberg has given us a world of the kind we used to find in the great novels, and, that it casts a spell. One forgets that these were, and some still are, living people who walked the earth, for the book envelops us in so authentic an atmosphere that the actualities of time and space die down, and another existence, that of eternity, takes its place. Even the cobblestones of the old streets in Kansas City have their echoes, as does the very grass and sky, and the dinginess of the back-parlor, where Lizzie heats soup in a battered kettle for her squeamish, delicate but remarkably enduring son, is no more than the mirrored light of countless scenes which most modern fiction would have us forget. The very image of a whole woman, sensual, pining, mistaken and utterly appealing in her unworldly attempts to battle with the world is, by this time, a novel event. One even forgets that the son, who flees the mother to find himself, and returns to the mother to beseech for the unknown father, and who must invoke the dream for revelation, is the author, and not the fable. For the fable takes over, as the dream enlightens the author, and the magic of an experience that sought the dark to find the light, casts its mighty spell.

Because I Was Flesh is a great achievement, and, as the culmination of a long, arduous, dedicated, creative venture during which the contraries, the irascible, the didactic were finally reconciled with the *Amor Fati* of acceptance, it is also a triumph.

ALFRED KAZIN

THE ELOQUENCE OF FAILURE

IN THE NINETEEN THIRTIES Edward Dahlberg published his own story several times in the form of fiction—*Bottom Dogs,* published with an introduction by D. H. Lawrence; *From Flushing to Calvary; Those Who Perish.* The last of these autobiographical novels of the lower depths in America came out in 1934, and then in 1941, beginning with a work of criticism, *Do These Bones Live,* Dahlberg became a fretful *avant-garde* all by himself, crankily learned, complicated, orphic, and arrogant. Yet after many years he has come back as an autobiographer to the story he told first as a novelist.

The analogy with Hemingway's posthumous memoir, *A Moveable Feast,* is startling and ironic. For Hemingway was able to write one of his very best books in *A Moveable Feast* because he consciously reused material that he had practiced to perfection in his stories. By directly confronting certain poignant episodes in his early Paris days with the assurance, subtlety, and ease of his long training, he was able to bring off a remarkable performance despite all the moral sleight-of-hand involved in writing autobiography for the sake of narrative—a form that permits the freedom of fiction under the covering of fact. Hemingway was writing, as only Americans do with so much feeling, to exculpate himself from the guilt attached to success. The subject of *A Moveable Feast* is the innocence that was lost by experience and that can be reclaimed, Hemingway thought, by the active creative voice of the accomplished writer chanting its youthful exultations.

111

Edward Dahlberg, who was born in 1900, a year after Hemingway, also grew up in the Middle West. None of his books, whether the social-realist novels of the 1930's or the "wisdom" books of the 1940's, has sold anything to speak of. He is one of the last true expatriates (in Mallorca) and uncompromising holdouts on the subject of America the expensive and unbeautiful, confident that if an old-fashioned literary rebel like himself holds onto his papers, they will be bought by the libraries of universities where assistant professors can become associate professors by getting exclusive rights to footnote the solitaries, rebel experimenters, and misfits of the previous generation.

Dahlberg does not have the gift of success. Even *Because I Was Flesh*, which is easily his best book and sums up his life to transcend the extraordinary pain of it with one fierce creative act, has aroused the sympathetic wonder and admiration of many good writers without stirring the public that is now eagerly buying *A Moveable Feast*. Dahlberg writes now, as he has always written, against a background of failure. Hemingway in his autobiography went back to his youth in Paris in order to cover himself, as it were, with its purity and ardor; Dahlberg has gone back to his youth in Kansas City with a haunted, still unbelieving effort to master experiences to which all the rest of his life has been captive. After many years and many early tracings of the subject in his novels, Dahlberg still writes as if his prime need as a man and as a writer were to face his dispiriting memories. Despite the inflated style with which, since *Do These Bones Live*, he attempts to raise every observation to the grandeur of universal myth, Dahlberg's life has in fact been terrible, and in this book he relieves the terror with urgent passion. He has finally achieved his triumph as an artist by reconstituting the failure that always dogged him.

Dahlberg takes his stand on fact: his life has been like no one else's. People's lives are not commensurable. Yet because of general deprivation in his youth, represented to his mind as a kind of cultural hunger, loneliness, cast-offness, Dahlberg wants to put his experiences with the world's—to list his experience among the great myths. The reader of this extraordinary book finds himself held by Dahlberg's memory of his mother's Star Lady Barbershop in Kansas City at 16 E. 8th, under the old viaduct, among the sports and dudes and butter-and-egg men of the Teddy Roosevelt era. But Dahlberg's push into the past is always retrieved by an effort to pull himself up into what Whitman called the mythic universal— an effort to lift these hard rocks of poverty and lust and abortion up into the mythic world where, for Dahlberg, Abel and Cain, Orpheus and Prometheus, Ishmael and Hagar, Jesus and Mary become witnesses and commentators on his own fate.

Dahlberg's initial misfortune was an archaic and literary one: he was illegitimate. His mother, a Polish Jewish immigrant with an oddly Swedish maiden name (originally Dalberg), had deserted her husband and two children to run off with a handsome villain named Saul, a fanatic for sexual pleasure who departed before his son was born in Charity Hospital in Boston and who came back only when he needed money or a temporary refuge. The mother, barely five feet tall, who wandered about the country with the boy until she was able to start her own business as a lady barber in Kansas City, became the greatest single fact in his life. A sense of common misfortune united mother and son; her hysterically tireless efforts to keep afloat, to find a husband for herself and so become respectable, were naturally translated by the son into a conviction of his own unlucky destiny and his distrust of a world in which other people had the money and high spirits.

Despite Dahlberg's many invocations of Kansas City as a lustful city and of the customers in his mother's barbershop as roaring bucks, the most authentic and impressive note in his book is of the unnaturalness, loneliness, and bareness of his confinement to his mother. While Hemingway's golden memories of Paris in the twenties are being relished by hundreds of thousands, it is understandable that readers in a time of anxious prosperity should overlook material that Dahlberg himself cannot record without a wild, just barely controlled pain. He writes, for example, of the end of a day with his mother:

When she closed up before midnight, she trudged home very slowly, as she did not want to spend a nickel for streetcar fare. She took deep breaths of the evening air and was overcome with a beating, upsurging confidence. As long as her lungs and heart were sound, she knew her future would be right. Her land-

113

lord, Wolforth, believed in her noble traits—since she always paid her rent on time. As she gazed at the maples along the street, she let out a sigh like that which had saved desponding Hagar in the wilderness.

Late in the evening, when every bone in her body ached, she would sometimes stop in a dark hallway to relieve herself; while she squatted there she told herself that she was the most miserable woman on earth. The boy walked a few paces ahead so as not to see her and also to watch for anybody who might be passing by. When he looked at the Milky Way, he would lift up his voice to the stars that were the lambs and stones of heaven, and heave a prayer out of his mouth to God, beseeching Him to give his mother a firm bladder so that she would not let out water in doorways, which he could not help hearing. Feeling easier, she walked up 8th Street to the flat, and when she heard a trolley on the tracks her courage came back to her.

The elevated reference to "Hagar in the wilderness" is as typical of Dahlberg as the poignant Dreiserian moment. Ever since the end of the 1930's, when Dahlberg withdrew from social realism by devouring the great scriptures and mythologies as if to inoculate himself against any danger from intellectual materialism in the future, he has made a point of dressing up his books with references to Ovid, Pliny, Luke, Jeremiah, Matthew, Mark, Sir Thomas Browne, Thoreau, and other sages. Dahlberg believes that the great writers can be therapists for those who suffer from invincible ignorance.

This mythification of experience works better in Dahlberg's autobiography than it does in dogmatic treatises like *Do These Bones Live, The Sorrows of Priapus*, and the frantic assaults on more successful twentieth-century writers that he put into the letters to Herbert Read published as *Truth Is More Sacred*. As a thinker in the abstract, Dahlberg is not very interesting; his own life is his most dependable text, and when he sees himself as Ishmael, it is because he has good reason to. Dahlberg writes out of a personal hell—spiritual, physical, cultural, and existentialist. He naturally feels close to the prototypes in the Bible of Jewish suffering, for he too has been exiled, lost in the desert, ground down, spat upon, with only a book, some wise book, to be his Law and his Prophets. There are times in this passionate recital when Sir Thomas Browne and even Thoreau—perhaps especially Thoreau, who managed without women—do not really help us to see better the Star Lady Barbershop, but they are there to make us see Dahlberg himself as a lofty, sage, and detached fellow. Yet the sheer truth of this man's life, because he finally does tell it, forces us to protect Dahlberg's innocent conceit. This kind of learning has been his life. He is very literary, and his chapter on the six years when his mother packed him off to the Jewish Orphan Society in Cleveland read as if those early memories had been dyed in a distillation of nineteenth-century orphanages. And when he describes his miseries as a hobo in 1919, the brutalities and sheer lunatic bad luck with which, for example, he thirstily fell upon what he took for a full keg of water in the Mojave Desert to find that he was drinking kerosene, or the blows of fate that rained down on him in Needles, California, you recognize how predestined and natural are his allusions to the Dead Sea, to Gehenna, to Gaza, and "the cinders and waste places of Jerusalem."

One of the most significant complaints in Dahlberg's book is his lamentation over the pitiless repetition of his experiences. He knows how little we can do to change ourselves; the brutal monotony of a single person's fears become for him the prison house in which all people live. At the end of his book he describes, against the background of his first disordered attempts to write, how his mother died in a New York slum. She had been cheated of all her hopes for a husband and protector, and when her son married and went away, she tried to keep death off by a conscious effort. Her son was away when she died; her body lay on a cot for five days before a neighbor found her. These last pages attain a beauty of truthfulness beyond anything I have read in recent American writing. The failure of Dahlberg's hopes speaks with eloquence to a society that has never been so prosperous or so afraid of poverty, failure, disease, unhappiness, anxiety, guilt. The book had to be written just now, when the times are more against Dahlberg than ever before. After so long a fight he looks better than he ever did: he writes better, he has more dignity, and he is more important to us all.

115

SIR HERBERT READ

FOREWORD TO *ALMS FOR OBLIVION*

I REMEMBER that early in my career as a writer an unknown well-wisher wrote and begged me to give up my critical activities and confine myself to the kind of literature for which my gifts were better suited, namely, imaginative literature. I was told I had an eye for concrete particulars and little ability in philosophical generalizations. I was reminded of this admonition when I read the first pages of Edward Dahlberg's essay on Allen Tate, for there he describes, if only obliquely, his own practice in criticism. It appears that he too has no love and perhaps little gift for "the mock elevated style of the philosopher and scientist," and yet this essay, and all the rest that comprise this volume, are nothing if not critical. We may therefore conclude that there are at least two methods of criticism. One we might call philosophical and the other, if a philosophical critic had not usurped the term, practical. Since practical criticism as a descriptive phrase has come to be associated with those "sophisters" and "noddies" who attempt "to find out what is in the poet's mind as he labors for precise numbers," we cannot very well use it to define Edward Dahlberg's kind of criticism (which is also the kind of Ben Jonson, Dryden, and Bagehot). I would call it "concrete" criticism, but Mr. Dahlberg would say that such a word belongs to "the jargon of aesthetics." His preference is to speak of auricular and sensual pleasures, and literature must first and foremost satisfy his "goatish appetite" for such phenomenal fodder. The pose is Gargantuan, and Rabelais is undoubtedly one of our author's monitors. Like Rabelais, he will list a hundred particulars, but never

117

risk a generalization. It is not possible to define pleasure or truth. "Since knowledge is chimerical, the academic stench is more horrid when the cabala of grammar is passed off as metaphysics." Since Mr. Dahlberg despises so many academic ideals—definition, analysis, syntax, the scientific method itself—it is little wonder that he is not honored in Academe, which is to say, not in any hall of renown, for nowadays they are all leased to pedants.

Mr. Dahlberg would describe himself merely as a humble reader, "rapt in love with" poetry and prose. His criticism when it ceases to be denunciatory, is confession. Some of the best of his pages are memories, and he would say that because style is the man himself, a knowledge of the man is a key to his style. His portraits of Dreiser, Anderson, and Ford Madox Ford tell us more about these authors, as authors, than a whole library of exegesis. Even the glimpse of Allen Tate's "wry, Poesque face flensed by some teleological anguish," tells us more about Tate's genius than the preceding references to his works. He does not write many words about Edmund Wilson or William Carlos Williams, but those words bite deeply and are indelible.

I should perhaps emulate the author's method in this tribute, but I doubt my skill. I have known him many years, in his joy and his suffering, and count myself lucky to have retained his respect and love, for he is a relentless scourge of all human frailties, especially those that threaten the integrity of the writer. He tells us (in this book) that what our genius lacks most is being simple, and though he is as ever thinking of style, the style is not separable from the way of life. He himself has always preferred to live simply, and his dwellings have been like the hermit's cell. I do not imply loneliness or lack of human contacts, for he enjoys good talk, despises the pervert, and believes that bad writing shows a lack of love. A poet, he says, "comes to the city to get his thoughts published, but there is always in him some wild Platte Dakota, or Rocky Mountain peak to resist the simpering vices of trade and deceit. Writing is conscience, scruple, and the farming of our ancestors." Typical that he should add this last phrase, but a poet concerned for style is likely to have a stronger sense of social values than the styleless sociologue. This poet believes (as I do) that "unless we return to the old handicrafts, to the wheat, stable, and horse village, to poems, houses, bricks, and tables, which are manual, we will become a nation of killers, for if people do not employ their hands in making what is good, or gentle, or noble, they will be criminals." Edward Dahlberg's criticism is a protest against our universal condition of alienation, which is our condition of damnation, and it is little wonder that the damned turn away from its revelation of their condition.

Sunset, he says on another page, "has fallen upon American letters, though it is less than a hundred years ago that we had a meadowy, daybreak verse and essay. It looked as though we were on the verge of some unusual sunrise; the land was pasture; Thoreau's *Walden* was a woodland lesson and prayer in how to live without wasting the human spirit." Those moving words give us the essence of the man and his message. Here, as everywhere, he fulfills his own ideal—his style is another name for his perception and his wisdom.

That perception and that wisdom culminate in the most direct and surprising contradiction of accepted values in his essay on Melville. I confess I had always shared the common admiration for Melville's allegorical epic, but never was an illusion of mine so immediately shattered. Of course, many American critics will come to the rescue of a work of such decisive import for the myth of an American literature, but Mr. Dahlberg takes his stand on what is most central to literature of any kind, the language, and he has no difficulty in showing that *Moby-Dick* is "shabbily written." He makes concessions, to the style as well as to social relevance, but in the end there is no escaping the conclusion that *Moby-Dick* is "a book of monotonous and unrelenting gloom." The gloom would not matter, and the monotony is relieved by such miraculous images as the one rescued from the gloom by Mr. Dahlberg himself—"the currents carry ye to those sweet Antilles where the beaches are only beat with water-lilies." It is conceded that Melville had enough genius to sing on occasion (our author cites a further litany of "canorous lines"), but they are not enough to save Melville's vessel from the weight of his indignation.

It should be noted, however, that this indignation is fundamen-

119

tally moral. What Mr. Dahlberg objects to most strongly in Melville is his misogamy. "There is no doxy, trollop, or trull in any of Melville's volumes . . . The hatred of women is the pederastic nausea that comes from the mention of the womb . . . Melville, Whitman, Poe, and Thoreau loathed the female, and the first three sages suffered from sodomy of the heart." Such intellectual sodomy ("as gross and abundant today as sexual perversion") is the burden of much of Edward Dahlberg's criticism, and it comes from his conviction that such "pathic" elements in modern literature come from "the refusal to be simple about plain matters." We return, therefore, to the test of style, and by always returning to this test, by insisting on very little else, Mr. Dahlberg becomes a critic of a most salutary kind. His judgments are severe, but they are motivated by a conviction he shares with Henry James, namely, "the very obvious truth that the deepest quality of a work of art will always be the quality of the mind of the producer." The moral sense and the artistic sense, as James observed on the same occasion, lie very near together, and it is Edward Dahlberg's distinction, in an age that has largely forgotten, if it ever heeded this admonition, to have reminded us of its obvious truth.

120

FRANK MACSHANE

TWO REVIEWS:

I. *Alms for Oblivion* AND OTHERS

SINCE THE APPEARANCE of his autobiography in 1964, Edward Dahlberg has published three new works, *Alms for Oblivion*, a collection of critical writings, *Reasons of the Heart*, a book of maxims and *Cipango's Hinder Door*, a volume of verse. Together, these books exemplify Dahlberg's position and importance as a literary figure. The autobiographical *Because I Was Flesh* had already revealed his rich and varied personal history. His childhood adventures as the son of a lady barber in Kansas City, his adolescence in a Cleveland orphanage and his young manhood as an itinerant scholar in California and New York all helped create an individual very much at odds with the world. When he began to write, he naturally used his experiences for purpose of social protest, but eventually he came to realize that they had overtones that went far beyond his anger with bourgeois values. He saw that his adventures were like those of many self-reliant orphans in classical Greece and medieval Spain who for centuries had learned to live by their wits and thereby gain knowledge and understanding of the world. In *Because I Was Flesh* Dahlberg presented his own experiences in the framework of this legendary and picaresque tradition and thus achieved a meaning and richness that far exceed the mere facts of his story.

But since *Because I Was Flesh* deals only with the early years of

121

Dahlberg's life, it gives little idea of his literary training or opinions. The earlier books, *Can These Bones Live* and *The Sorrows of Priapus*, are of some help in filling the gap, but as personally impressionistic observations and criticism, they are exploratory and tentative rather than definitive.

Of the three new books written some years later, *Alms for Oblivion* is the most helpful in defining Dahlberg's position as a writer. A collection of literary essays, memoirs and social criticism, it is unified by a consistent attitude towards art and letters. The writers admired—Dreiser, Anderson, Ford, Lawrence and Tate, all of them personal friends of the author—have the common quality of being men of feeling and compassion. "One does not have to be afraid of a meadow, which won't hurt you," writes Dahlberg; "what is to be dreaded is the mind without feeling, for it is a most malignant faculty." Human involvement is what makes a man and a writer: "Touch is our misery, our disgrace and our knowledge." To clarify his position, Dahlberg lists those he scorns, the heartless writers like Melville, James, Fitzgerald, and Hemingway who are all solitaries, denying their mothers and fathers, brothers and wives. That these are the most influential and dominant writers in America today is for Dahlberg but a rueful commentary on the times. Unable to communicate with their fellow human beings, these men placed a compensatory reliance on things, especially money. By contrast, writes Dahlberg, "Anderson cowered before money, fearing it might destroy what was fecund in him."

Dahlberg recognizes that this strain of isolated individualism has been dominant in American literature. Thoreau, Poe, Melville, Mark Twain, Whitman, and James were all lonely men, several of them bachelors, whose work dealt with public or social subjects rather than the affairs of the heart and the hearth. Dahlberg considers that what unites these writers is what he calls "the watery element"; and by that he does not mean merely that they wrote about Walden Pond or the Pacific Ocean or the Mississippi, but that as "a plethora of water in the spirit destroys filial affection," so this quality also induces frigidity. As he says elsewhere, ". . . our most gifted writers have too much seawater in their heads, and all of them were cold men." The instability that comes with anything based on flux and movement has meant that our national literature "is exceedingly poor in victuals and amours."

For Dahlberg this is the great weakness of American letters. "There is no doxy, trollop, or trull in any of Melville's volumes," he says, meaning in effect that our writers seem incapable of dealing successfully with the full varieties of domestic life. Our Shakespeare is O'Neill, our Cervantes Mark Twain, our Fielding is James, our Keats Poe, and our Homer is the solitary singer of Camden. For Dahlberg, in short, literature should be concerned with human beings: "Born to sin because we have genital organs, we live to confess our faults, and that is scripture and literature." Thus, too, we must turn to the land, the element that supports our being: "Speech, to be a deity to the people, must come from the pasture or from grain, fruits, and livestock." What underlies this preference for the solid as against the fluctuating is a desire for self-knowledge. This is really the end of art for Dahlberg, and one that can come only through stability and human involvement, rather than through the isolation of wandering men like Melville, of whom Dahlberg writes, "A novelist, he had almost no knowledge of people. What we call knowledge of others is what we know about ourselves."

Dahlberg's position, as revealed in this collection of essays on Anderson, Dreiser, and Stieglitz, Robert McAlmon and Randolph Bourne, Melville and Allen Tate, is coherent and clear. Moreover, it has nonliterary overtones. When he writes, "Sunset has fallen upon American letters, though it is less than a hundred years ago that we had a meadowy, daybreak verse and essay," he is not merely mourning the condition of contemporary literature, he is bemoaning the very condition of modern life. "I think we are more afraid of being near each other," he concludes the same paragraph, "than committing some dark vice." Not surprisingly, Dahlberg places a good deal of the blame on urbanization, noting for example, that Sherwood Anderson "is insubstantial whenever he departs from the cornfields" and that Dreiser's genius would have perished had he not been a Hoosier. Like Thoreau, Dahlberg hearkens back to eighteenth century rural simplicity because "The world we live in does not belong to us, and it has made us wild, city waifs. . . .

123

What is cold and inhuman has seeped down into the market, the store, and into poetry. . . . The grim coffin faces behind counters are like Pilate who was always washing his hands. . . . We are so clever that we are fast dying from it. . . . Engineers, mechanics, college professors, we are no longer a manual people." These observations may seem to suggest that Dahlberg is merely an escapist, a person so unreconciled to modern life that he finds solace only in anachronistic disavowal.

While there is some justification for this suspicion, since by temperament Dahlberg seems to have an aversion to contemporary life, his words do not merely represent a private self-indulgence. Certain remarks easily transcend sentimental recall: "The plough is a sign of peaceable ground-workers," he writes, "but the rubber tire is a tool of a nomadic, apathetic class that is constantly moving away from debts, marriage, and boredom." Moreover, Dahlberg is not interested in sociological homilies for their own sake: industrialism is no mere nuisance, it is an absolute threat to survival. "This is a corrosive, war-nerve culture," he writes, "and not an era of love and human adhesion. The industrial city . . . exhausts and stupefies the multitude. . . . War is the health of the state . . . [and] . . . our vast, wild production is the invidious battle material by which we enslave the people at home and defeat the oppressor abroad." This last notion is one inherited from Randolph Bourne who during the first World War badgered the authorities with remarks as prescient as some of those currently directed towards President Johnson.

A reading of *Alms for Oblivion* thus inevitably forces us to Stanley Kunitz's recent comment on Dahlberg: "We had better stop thinking of him as a literary curiosity and pay attention to his voice. Edward Dahlberg is nourished by a great rage." The prophet-like utterances that characterize Dahlberg's two other new books, *Reasons of the Heart* and *Cipango's Hinder Door*, derive to a certain extent from his conviction that America desperately needs a sense of direction and order. "No people require maxims so much as the American," he writes. "The reason is obvious: the country is so vast, the people always going somewhere, from Oregon apple valley to boreal New England, that we do not know whether to be temperate orchards or sterile climate. Great cultures come out of small Homeric or Hebraic lands. . . . What our genius lacks most is being simple." Dahlberg believes that this naturalness and sense of identity cannot be obtained through mere description. "Our literature lacks maxims and proverbs," he observes; "cartography takes the place of the intellectual faculty."

Dahlberg's decision to compile an intellectually vigorous book of this sort may nevertheless seem anomalous. By nature, the aphoristic utterance seems alien in a society which likes to be shown but does not like to be told what life is like. The pithiness that characterizes most aphoristic generalizations also appears to be more in keeping with the witty discourse of the eighteenth century than with the flaccid jargon of our own times. Yet Dahlberg's decision to follow in the footsteps of Hippocrates, Heraclitus, Pascal, and La-Rochefoucauld was caused in part by a strong belief in language as a moral weapon. "A good remark uttered in cumbersome words feebly put together is evil," he observes. "Not one wise thought can be told without great energy. When the will languishes, the demons are triumphant."

Reasons of the Heart covers a number of subjects, ranged under headings like "Wisdom and Folly" and "Time and Death" as well as dealing with domestic topics like food, sleep, and dreams. These categories are mere conveniences, however, for throughout, the voice is consistent. Among the best, scattered throughout the volume, are the maxims dealing with the strange instability of human behavior: "If you are looking for an enemy be kind, gentle and above all truthful." "He who tells you he is very busy implies that you are a wastrel." "Whenever a man confesses he is a failure he is sorely disappointed if nobody contradicts him." "He who claims to be just has a granite bosom." "I have no confidence in a man whose faults you cannot see." "Pitiless is the man who alleges he is sensitive." Dahlberg also makes general observations on literature and society as in "Beauty has been replaced by the rubble and cement gods, and the venerated altars are the shops filled with the Three Fatal Disgraces, Plastic, Rubber and Petrol."

Still, the most interesting maxims are those that reveal Dahlberg's awareness of the sad contradictions of ordinary human life.

125

Some of the best attain an almost tragic intensity: "The older one grows the more he doubts that he was ever alive." "The simplest way of living as a solitary is to tell people where you are." "One needs a windfall every day to be sociable." In dealing with these more suggestive aspects of behavior, Dahlberg does not restrict himself to the brief aphorism but frequently employs a discursive and reflective statement as well, so that some of the maxims extend to full paragraphs.

Similar variations of mood and temperament occur in Dahlberg's most recent book, a collection of verse called *Cipango's Hinder Door*. This book also contains aphorisms and prose passages which appear between sections of blank verse. This distinction of forms is not disruptive, however, for Dahlberg's verse is all of a piece, the product, as Allen Tate writes in his admirable introduction to the poems, of a "unified intelligence."

In subject matter, the book moves from the general to the particular, opening with the title poem which deals with America as a whole—the Cipango, or Japan, towards which, having read Marco Polo's account of his travels, Christopher Columbus thought he was sailing. In lines that draw heavily upon history and legend, Dahlberg traces the conjunction of the ancient races of Europe with the Indian civilizations of America. As Dahlberg sees it, this meeting involved the encounter of a deeply domestic civilization, one known for its humane customs and artistic achievement, not with the fabulous East of cinnamon and pepper that had fascinated the Venetians, but with a stark and stony civilization of millet and maize, typified by human sacrifices and gold-embossed daggers. From this bloody conjunction came no new race of whole men, but rather a lonely and exacerbated people. The brand of Cain thus implanted in American soil by a people unable to reconcile opposites forced the new race of transplanted Europeans to take refuge in an absolutist rationalism. The civilization of modern America is therefore inevitably eclectic and disjointed, producing a dissatisfied people given to violence and vulgarity.

Most of the poems which encompass this vision of the hemisphere are fairly long. Drawing upon mythology, literature, and the physical landscape, Dahlberg attempts to evoke the historical figures themselves, rather in the manner of certain books of the Old Testament where cataloguing of names is intermingled with prophecy and the narration of historical events. Dahlberg's poems have something in common with Whitman's, but the range of subjects is less wide than that of *Song of Myself*; instead, they aim for the kind of immediacy achieved in William Carlos Williams' *In the American Grain*, a book much admired by Dahlberg.

Yet in truth the short lyrics which close the book are those to which the reader is most likely to return. Free of what in some of the longer poems seems learning heavily worn, these lyrics have an emotional intensity that derives from actual experience. The following lines are typical of this section:

> I am galled and stung and wonder why.
> I am genial by accident,
> Gray and hulled as the sea at noon,
> And by evening rueful as a ditch
> With no twilight to salve my bruised gorge.
> When I am in the sun
> The arrows of the moon pierce my bosom.
> I put on the colors of my nature
> As a woman her powder and paint,
> And would not know I was bad or choleric
> Were there no people to affect my spleen.
> Were there no persons in the earth
> I would have no faults.
> I could be content to embrace a rock, a precipice or a
>   ravine,
> Could I do without others.
> Were I a sandy bank,
> Or were there bedrock to bottom my identity,
> I would not be my own enemy.

Here the words, though natural and free, are imbued with Dahlberg's deep reading. The experience is immediate, but gains significance for having passed through Dahlberg's literary system.

What finally do these three books tell us of Edward Dahlberg and what is their importance in contemporary American letters? The first part of any answer must acknowledge how far Dahlberg is from the current orthodoxy of the literary papers and journals. Wholly unconcerned with the topical and trivial, he is interested only in the fundamentals of human life. Of these he speaks with an openness that recalls the work of Whitman, Dreiser, and Lawrence. He writes from the inside with the conviction that a man's writing must be consistent with his nature. This moral attitude might seem to limit Dahlberg as a writer, for there is always something harsh and disagreeable in the prophet with glittering eyes. Yet his best work is always sympathetic: his first-rate literary intelligence, which is his gift and achievement, redeems him. Thus in one of his poems he writes: "Water is death, but man must seek it." With Dostoyevsky Dahlberg acknowledges that whereas in morals two plus two equals four, in art, they always total five. In part, Dahlberg's significance derives from his attempt to reconcile the two, knowing all along that his task is impossible. "We cannot put upon a poet a creed or religion," he writes, "but he must have one character or we will have the most dreary pluralistic morals, a moral for every new occasion." These three books demonstrate the range and consistency of this literary character, one that is absolutely unique in modern America.

II. A Man On His Own

In his equivocal introduction to Edward Dahlberg's *Bottom Dogs*, D. H. Lawrence offered a statement of advice: "I don't want to read any more books like this. But I am glad to have read this one, just to know what is the last word in repulsive consciousness, consciousness in a state of repulsion." What Lawrence objected to in 1929 was Dahlberg's ruthless portrayal of society as loveless and rootless. Dahlberg himself, in his disavowal of the novel in its 1961 paperback edition, thought the fault lay with its style: "The defect of the novel lies in its jargon," he wrote, in its use of "the rude American vernacular."

As Josephine Herbst has pointed out, the book has both faults: it is limited and uneven in both form and substance. But Dahlberg did not immediately accept Lawrence's advice; for two more novels

128

he pursued the chimera of proletarian naturalism and wrote literary journalism. Then, quite suddenly, he stopped. "I know I have made many craven errors," he wrote Allen Tate in a letter printed in *Epitaphs of Our Times,* "and I resolved as early as '34 to be a man of letters, and to be an eremite to do so." He withdrew from the literary community, leaving behind him a score of estranged left-wing colleagues who tried to make his removal permanent. For nearly 20 years Dahlberg remained in limbo, hardly writing at all, but reading constantly in the works of the ancients and preparing himself for a new literary career. Now this long apprenticeship is over, and Dahlberg has published seven books within the last four years, three of them this year. With most of his contemporaries fallen into silence, Dahlberg in his sixties has emerged as the most productive writer of his generation.

A number of themes are clearly revealed in this recent work. One of these is his belief in the primacy of substance over form. Dahlberg rejects the fashionable theory that literary technique can serve as a guide to moral values. While recognizing the wit and cleverness of writers like Wilde and Joyce, he also perceives their falseness. Of Wilde's "To regret one's own experience is to arrest one's own development," Dahlberg observes: "It is a clever remark and one has to give it very close thought to see how wrong it is." By way of contrast, Dahlberg states that the Flemish painter Hieronymus Bosch "is great because what he imagines in color can be translated into justice."

For Dahlberg, artistry can evolve only from imaginative perceptions and vigorous thought. "We are astonished by Homer because he writes as Achilles casts the spear of Pelion ash. Every verb should have that epical and martial force."

Dahlberg also relies on the history and literature of the past to enrich his style and justify his opinions. Knowledge of this kind can keep a writer from being entrapped in his immediate surroundings, and Dahlberg rejoices that he "never lost connection with the European mind. Of course, everything American is in my marrow, a tree, a ravine, sumac, the Rockies, but unless I know the experiences of Attica and Rome, what else can I be except a provincial scribbler?" History and the literature of the past also bring self-knowledge. "Go to school with some master," he advises Isabella Gardner, "Ovid, Plutarch, Livy, Tacitus, and you will then find the river back to your own identity."

These opinions help explain Dahlberg's mistrust of the vernacular and his fear of being enslaved by the usages of his own times. "I have no quarrel with naturalism as such," he told Theodore Dreiser in 1938, "but I want a purifactory naturalism."

For Dahlberg, writing is, as he says, a means "to understand myself a little better and to have friends." He believes that as friendship can come only from a generous heart, so good writing requires an open and balanced spirit. "Character is fate and that's what writes the books, not grammar, not being clever, or imagining that one is the lion or the fox." Dahlberg's aim is for wholeness in literature as in life: "When the body is false unto itself, the intellect is a liar."

Dahlberg's views extend naturally to society in general. Two passages from a letter to Robert M. Hutchins directly relate art to public life:

"A writer should employ a language that can pierce the heart or awaken the mind. Style ought to have some kinship with mountains, seas, glens, orchards, furrows, if it is to have a symbolic and human value . . .

"There has to be love in a book if it is to be useful to society. 'Affection is the energy of society,' says Aristotle. And there also has to be people or a strong and pungent sense of them in words which we employ to persuade others. I find, however, the academic vocabulary is as peopleless as our commonwealth. You have walked along the streets of our modern cement towns, and seen nothing but houses with shades drawn, and gazed with a desponding wonder at our machine-made buildings and synthetic and fraudulent colonial dwellings. No one sits on the porch, which has vanished from our lives, and where American families sat in the dusk or in cool Indian summer evenings. Now you see no one, nothing but a few miserable tin cars squatting next to the curbstone."

Dahlberg's views, so eloquently expressed in this passage, have placed him in opposition to many of the pervasive tendencies of contemporary literature. Unlike Hemingway, who produced a

130

specifically American literature, Dahlberg feels that literary nationalism is mere provincialism. He is also opposed to literature that reproduces the chaos of contemporary life, and he therefore rejects the work of Joyce, Pound and Eliot. In a letter to Sir Herbert Read, he remarks: "The more of the world there is in a sentence, the less character there can be." Elsewhere he observes that "a truthful writer" tries neither to be simple nor difficult. "You have an unknown audience, and your only concern is to be honest in good, just words."

Other tendencies in contemporary art offend him. One of these is abstractionism, especially in painting. Dahlberg dislikes modern painting because it is merely "the lazy, sensual pleasure of the eyes. It is like music today, it makes the ears heavy and the mind sluggish." Conversely, literature or arts that have specific social aims, such as racial integration, are also incomplete and misdirected. "I would rather write a truthful book which might fall into the hands of two Negroes than pass another law giving this unfortunate people the right to vote in savage Mississippi," he notes to Josephine Herbst, for "the bottom of the misery is not the Negro, it is America . . . To be short, if one is to compose a poem to persuade the American to liberate the Negro, he has to compose it in a language of symbols and myths that will free the white American who is ready to emancipate the black one."

Consistent with Dahlberg's celebration of wholeness is his distaste for homosexuality and the mother-hatred which usually accompanies it. Dahlberg has long been conscious of the weakness of the female in American literature. The doleful heritage of the puritans has kept women of flesh and blood from the works of Poe, Whitman, Emerson and Melville, not to mention James, Hart Crane, Eliot and Pound. Hawthorne's Hester Prynne may have been a true woman, but the pervading atmosphere of *The Scarlet Letter* is one of sin and guilt. Thoreau, otherwise a favorite of Dahlberg's, was an icy bachelor.

Ignoring the intuition and warmth of the female spirit, utilitarianism and technology have taken control of American life. Dahlberg's attacks on modern conditions are some of the most memorable passages in his writings. Here are a few sentences on the ubiquitous supermarket: "Go into one of those vast sepulchral markets, where people hardly talk to one another, and where self-service prevails, and you quit it more wormy than Lazarus. After one has bought canned peas, or pallid, storage carrots wrapped in cellophane as the dead Pharaohs were garmented in papyri, you go to the cashier. Often a sour, wordless man or woman drops the coins into the palm of your hand so as not to touch it. But unless we exchange human germs, or otherwise we dare not kiss our mother, father or wife, we will expire, diseased and cankered, in absolute solitude."

Dahlberg's rejection of his own times is much like Thoreau's. He is a nay-sayer only because he loves his country. Anger and misanthropy are different, for as Dahlberg remarks in a letter to Karl Shapiro: "Do you take a weak affirmation when there is a strong negation that is better? . . . I am by nature an iconoclast, but one who is always in search of images, fables and proverbs—the wine for the aching heart."

The accusation of being out of date and anachronistic Dahlberg accepts without demur: "As for myself, I am a medievalist," he wrote Sherwood Anderson nearly 30 years ago, "a horse and buggy American, a barbarian, anything that can bring me back to the communal song of labor, sky, star, field, love." Dahlberg has no belief in progress. In *The Leafless American* he makes this comparison: "The difference between the Roman and the American empire is that we are now adopting the licentious habits of a Poppaea or a Commodus, or a Domitian, without having first acquired stable customs, deities, or a civilization. And we are about to become a soldier nation without any real knowledge of Europe, Asia or the Orient."

For the most part, Dahlberg's negations are based on positive values. These are the old values of family, the land, ancient wisdom, animals and good prose, whose qualities he celebrates in order to cure the ills of the nation and avert its destruction. At this level, he is an activist. As he wrote Sir Herbert Read: "I must then say that knowledge that is not action is gross and evil."

The three books under review reveal Dahlberg's range as a writer. What unites them is the extraordinary quality of their

132

prose, which can only have developed from an abundant understanding of life. The finest parts of *The Edward Dahlberg Reader* are extracts from the autobiographical *Because I Was Flesh*. Here the raw experience of *Bottom Dogs* is transformed into literature, for Dahlberg has successfully followed his own advice to Isabella Gardner: "You must find a language for your feelings, warm and good, to transfigure them."

Fortunately, the editor has included the touchingly humorous section of this book that deals with the courtship of his mother by Tobias Emeritch, surely one of the gloomiest figures in American literature, in rain or sunshine wrapped in his muffler and encased in an overcoat and rubber galoshes. The dialogue between them— Lizzie Dahlberg's animal vitality opposing the despairing pessimism of Tobias—reproduces fundamental strains in Dahlberg's own character. His imaginative genius consists in the skill with which he brings these characteristics to life.

The Leafless American contains essays, book reviews and poems that have not previously been published in book form. Its exceptional range makes it a useful complement to the *Reader*.

Epitaphs of Our Times is sure to attract many readers, as much for its immediate revelation of Dahlberg's powerful character as for the intense prose in which the letters are written. I know of no American collection that deals more directly with writing and with the fundamental issues of literature. As passionate as Keats's letters, Dahlberg's have the massive variety and control of Flaubert's.

Addressed to 15 individuals, most of them writers, these letters not only chronicle the past 30 years, they are also a series of essays on contemporary life and literature. The letters to Robert M. Hutchins deal with the function of the arts in society; those to Sir Herbert Read are concerned with the correct posture for a man of letters today. The letters to Isabella Gardner and Stanley Burnshaw reveal Dahlberg as a literary mentor. William Carlos Williams, Allen Tate and others are biographical documents of Dahlberg's own penury and neglect over the past decade.

Edward Dahlberg is handsomely revealed in these three volumes as easily the most remarkable writer in America today.

Robert Kindrick

THE BENEVOLENT SCOURGE: EDWARD DAHLBERG
AND MODERN AMERICAN LETTERS

AT PRESENT, much of American literature is produced by writers of two different orders. The university poets and critics from Chicago and Vanderbilt and their successors have dominated the bookshelves of America's literary elite. This modern marriage of Parnassus and academia has provided a financial shelter and a respectable career for many artists. Very often, however, such writers produce emasculated criticism and impotent fiction. Only a few men such as Allen Tate, John Crowe Ransom, and Robert Penn Warren have managed to escape the castration of academic havens.

Many of our younger avant-garde writers have fared little better. Having consciously divorced themselves from the sterility of the academics, they have also neglected the important traditions of letters. Moreover, the development of the pragmatic aesthetic, which measures the value of experience not by its morality but by its intensity, has led these writers to concern themselves with drugs, homosexuality, and satanism. Their literary interests have been determined by the tendency of criticism since, say, 1920, to praise not what is good but what is different. The results of their attempts to transcend what they consider the clichés of living are unfortunate. For these men and women, the obligation of the writer to truth and beauty has disappeared, and we are presented with books which contain little more than scrawled neuroses.

Some of our most important modern American writers are members of neither of these camps. Edward Dahlberg is such a writer without a discernible commitment to the dogma of either group. Although he has been a teacher, Mr. Dahlberg is not an academic prig. Although he has been "on the road" he has not indulged in the excesses of our bohemian litterateurs. Any member of the American community of letters has a three-fold debt to this neglected seer. Ignored or berated even until the late 1950's, Dahlberg has enriched American language and literature in his special linguistic interests, his contributions to fiction and creative writing, and his literary criticism.

Edward Dahlberg's linguistic concerns evidence his reverence for the language of past English masters. The way that he uses language is not as the chic modern who seems to disregard linguistic forms in his search for the different. Dahlberg does not eschew syntax and scatter his words in meaningless patterns; he does not stretch the laws of definition to their furthest limits; and he feels no obligation to deal with dry and hackneyed commonplaces as startling new materials. He does not attempt to strain language to recapture a means of communication; rather he has gone to an opposite pole. By his particular concern for the fabric of language and the precise usage of his literary ancestors, he has developed an idiom more viable than most in our modern novels.

In a very simplistic form, the problem he and all 20th century writers have faced is this: In using words how is it possible to escape the wretched conglomeration of imprecise meanings which have developed around them through inaccurate usage and unclear thinking? How can the flat commonplaces of modern language be revivified into a workable literary idiom? How, in short, can the literary creator find an adequate linguistic tool? Stein, Hemingway, and Anderson (and initially Dahlberg in his *Bottom Dogs*) chose to work with the American vernacular and attempted to make the language more virile by the kind of special linguistic techniques mentioned above. Stein, indeed, found she had to write a new grammar to make her methods clear, and this is how she appraised the crucial problem:

Words have to do everything in poetry and prose and some writers write more in articles and prepositions and some say you should write in nouns, and of course one has to think of everything.

It has been Dahlberg's creative task, then, to find a way to make words do everything. He made a start (which he himself now considers a false start) in *Bottom Dogs* with the rough idiom he had learned in the Cleveland orphanage and the Kansas City streets. He worked carefully with the kinds of techniques which Dreiser, Anderson, and Stein developed, and as a result he wrote a book of remarkable interest. Dahlberg was at this time in the avant-garde of the proletarian writers, and his language was the vernacular of the working class. The common language in which Dahlberg described his rough experience caused D. H. Lawrence to comment:

It is a genuine book, as far as it goes, even if it is an objectionable one. It is in psychic disintegration, a good many stages ahead of *Point Counter Point*. It reveals a condition that not many of us have reached, but towards which the trend of consciousness is taking us, all of us, especially the young.

Yet Dahlberg repudiated this book and this attempt to find a workable literary instrument. After *From Flushing to Calvary*, and *Those Who Perish*, he returned with *Do These Bones Live* in the early '40's. The premises of his search for a viable linguistic medium had changed and he had evolved a style unique in the 20th century. Dahlberg, unlike many of his contemporaries, had found the answer to the problem of communication in past idioms and in a new conception of the fabric of language. He recently explained his attitutes toward language and usage in response to an *Arion* questionnaire on the modern value of the classics:

La Fontaine alleged that he who loved his own age more than ancient times was insane. Having his veneration for the past, I am not prepared to knock down an olden writer. Fowler has never been any advantage to me . . . If I am to learn anything about English—and this is my passion and despair—I can only do so by going to the Masters of that glorious language. Seeing how a word is used in a line by Dekker or Swift is a replenishing experience.

It is not, then, through cheap tricks with diction and syntax that Dahlberg hopes to infuse life into our modern parlance, but through the use of linguistic devices established by his great predecessors.

Dahlberg's veneration for the past and for the language of the great tradition has led him, then, to premises on the writer's task which he explained in the preface to the City Lights reissue of *Bottom Dogs*:

> The harm done to the English language has been immense; imagine anyone composing one of the great *Pensées* of Pascal in an abominable tongue; the adages in the *Haiku* are written in a savory language. Spirit is as imponderable as light and the raiment thereof are the lilies or the words that are dearer to us than Solomon's robes. Vile words come from the rabble; wit can be ribald though as well-lettered as Congreve's or Wycherley's plays.

Two of the ideas here are of the utmost importance in understanding Dahlberg's style. First, as the linguists were once prone to tell us, language may be considered a fabric, but it is not one that can be folded and twisted without damage. Indeed, for Dahlberg, it can be rent and destroyed by the irresponsible jugglings of pseudo-literary scribblers (and here he seems to condemn his own early work) and the imprecise usage of those who are unconcerned. For him, this severely limits the kinds of techniques which can be legitimately employed to find a viable style.

Secondly, Dahlberg is very much aware that language is the raiment of thought, and that base language indicates base thought. Here he is not talking simply about the kind of baseness that we associate with obscenity, although that is certainly at issue. He is also concerned with the baseness of the idiom that he and other proletarian writers used in the '30's, the baseness which our modern literature has inherited and which results in abjuring the full potential of our great linguistic legacy. It is interesting to note that modern psycholinguistics, in the work of Roger Brown and Jerome Bruner, is moving toward the same kind of premise which Dahlberg evolved out of his craftsmanship.

With these two premises, then, Dahlberg has turned for his new idiom not to the language of the street or the jargon of the academy, but to the virile prose of the 17th century. As Sir Herbert Read has noted, Dahlberg has tapped the "crystalline vein of the English Bible, of Shakespeare, and Sir Thomas Browne . . ." and he has found a means of washing away the linguistic rubbish with which we have burdened our modern lexicon. In seeking to get beyond the blandness and confusion of our modern tongue he has turned to an earlier and more vital prose instead of attempting the possibly hopeless task of purging our current idiom of its impurities. Moreover, he has broken with the generally paratactic prose which tends to dominate American fiction, and he has shown us that a hypotactic style is still both beautiful and functional.

Some modern scholars and critics have found Dahlberg's efforts distasteful; indeed, he has been called pretentious and misdirected. A style such as his may seem to them both archaic and abstruse. Yet, to berate Dahlberg because we cannot understand the direction of his efforts to solve the central linguistic problem of our time is to reveal our own ignorance. His stylistic devices are important if for no other reason than because they are unique in our age. Their singularity is not all that we should consider, however; in returning to an older and greater tradition in English letters for language with which to clothe his thought, Dahlberg has suggested a very efficacious alternative in our search for an adequate means of expression. While it is unlikely that our mass society will return to the simplicity of Elizabethan English, what Dahlberg has suggested is extremely important for the modern man of letters. In his effort to utilize the full resources of language, he has indicated how we may inject some vitality into our writing and thinking. We do not need more of the gadgeteering of modern poets and novelists, but more of the retrospection on our literary heritage which Dahlberg has provided.

The difference between the honest artist and the cheap peddler of letters is a Sisyphean effort to know and understand the hearts of men. Too often, however, our modern audiences have demanded sensationalism and the putrid residue of our cultural seaminess. Many of the most admired of our modern authors have won their undeserved reputations by showing us our own filth.

Edward Dahlberg has eschewed the base in our modern tradition, and he must have our respect for his achievement in American fiction. The magnitude of his contribution in ripening our literature is hard to gauge, but he has shown himself a true patron of culture. Here I wish to consider only two of his books, but I believe that through these two works we can partially measure Dahlberg's gift to the American republic.

Bottom Dogs, despite its creator's repudiation, is an important document in our literary history. Published in London in 1929 and in the United States in 1930, the book is truly a classic of its genre. Considerably better than most of its successors, the book is a landmark in American realism, and although it does not contain the best of Dahlberg's writing, it already evidences his commitment to complete honesty in his work.

Bottom Dogs is a harrowing account of life in America. In this book Dahlberg has included all of the bleakness and spiritual desiccation of the bottom dogs' life, and he has relentlessly forced on us the despair which his hero faced. In his introduction to the 1961 reissue, Dahlberg partially explained his intention in writing such a book:

> I had deliberately expunged some of the joys of this globe, sun, grass, river—the melons and the leeks for which the Israelites pined—in order not to write a slavish book about a society which concealed its filth and cruelty, and that doomed so many of its boys who became vagabonds, pariahs, or hopeless drudges in great cement cities. This sounds a little didactic, but first of all I wanted to tell a story, and maybe I did.

The character of the novel was deliberate. Dahlberg wanted us to face Lorry's hopelessness and he succeeded.

The book is exceptional in that Dahlberg met all the requirements of his genre, and despite the pessimism of the narrative, his ability to come to terms with his material is astounding. The description of Lorry's life in the orphanage, his trip west, and his stay at the Y.M.C.A., are all as uncompromising as Dahlberg's portrait of Mrs. Lewis and the barber shop:

140

Then when he saw his mother, her face, white with sweaty lines, like that old oily oilcloth he had to eat off on the table, he looked as though he had just found a fly in his soup. He didn't want to go back to that, watch his mother cook soup in black, sooty pots on that rusty, cockroachy gas range behind the shop; or try to eat his meat, while one of the barber girls, coming backshop in her haircutting apron, flushed the toilet, which was right next to the ice box, and whose wooden partition only rose halfway to the ceiling and had no roof.

In writing this book, Dahlberg employed techniques later associated with the proletarian writers of the 1930's, and he actually created a paradigm for the fiction of many other writers. Dahlberg himself now considers the book unfortunate, and in his classes he discourages his students from reading it.

It is significant that he began his introduction to the reissue with a quotation from Tolstoi: "Many men write books, but few are ashamed of them afterwards." Dahlberg was indeed ashamed afterwards, and his feelings are a mark of his literary integrity. Dahlberg now feels that in his early writing he was serving his artistic apprenticeship in public, and he has often stated that we should call no man a writer until after he is 50. For him perhaps only Shakespeare, "the Christ of literature," and Dean Swift wrote consistently well. Dahlberg would advise a man without the Jovian powers of these masters to burn his first works.

His disclaimer of *Bottom Dogs* is almost complete despite the book's importance. Yet it is a cenotaph in literary methods which have come to dominate much modern writing, and if we can find the reasons for Dahlberg's disavowal of this work, it may be easier to estimate his contribution to American letters in his later work.

Here I think D. H. Lawrence's comments in the introduction may be pertinent:

> Nothing I have ever read has astonished me more than the "Orphanage" chapters of this book. There I realized with amazement how rapidly the human psyche can strip itself of awareness and its emotional contacts, and reduce itself to a sub-brutal condition of simple gross persistence.

141

It is this "sub-brutal condition of simple gross persistence" that has come to dominate our modern literary heroes. We have exchanged our Hamlets and Rosalinds for Jason Compsons and Temple Drakes. It is partially this aspect of the novel to which Dahlberg objects.

Dahlberg has also exercised his own formidable critical powers to pick out defects in his early work. Besides decrying the simple brutishness of the characters, Dahlberg has stated, ". . . the defect of the novel lies in its jargon." Here Dahlberg has touched upon one of the key difficulties in earlier realistic writing and its modern heirs. In *Bottom Dogs* and its successors, the language is defective. And for Dahlberg the relation between language and thought is intimate—a book in a base parlance will have rough and brutal characters.

Between *Bottom Dogs* and *Do These Bone Live*, Dahlberg evolved a new view on language and rhetoric, and he became aware of a principle Allen Tate has stated in "Is Literary Criticism Possible?":

> By rhetoric I mean the study and the use of figurative language of experience as the discipline by means of which men govern their relations with one another in the light of truth.

Dahlberg's new conception of rhetoric also changed his ideas on the function of literature.

In *Because I Was Flesh* Dahlberg has remolded much of the material he initially presented in *Bottom Dogs*. It is an exceptional piece of writing. Using the "figurative language of experience" now, Dahlberg has given us his autobiography, but it is not full of the dull trivia that so often mar the writing of a Pepys or Evelyn. Once again Dahlberg has demonstrated his literary honesty, but in this work he has tried to encompass more of life than *Bottom Dogs* could hold. Allen Tate has used no hyperbole in his review when he states:

> A masterpiece. The hair-raising honesty, the profound self-knowledge, and the formal elegance of style are a combination that has not previously appeared in an autobiography by an American.

142

The book is filled with the wisdom Dahlberg has garnered from his long perspectives on experience; and it has lines of Elizabethan beauty: "It is hideous and coarse to assume that we can do something for others—and it is vile not to endeavor to do it." In this book Dahlberg's writing is enriched with the wisdom of all world literature. No longer are the simplistic theories of realism sufficient to order this excoriating experience, nor does he revel in the base. Dahlberg has abandoned our American concern for the crude, the vulgar, and the petty in life. In turning to Browne and Shakespeare for his idiom, he has also turned to the King James Bible, the Bhagavad-Gita, and Pascal's *Pensées* for his view of man. In *The Leafless American* Dahlberg tells us:

> Every vision has been patched together from the works of notable sages, and most books are a cento. When writing flags it means that people are forgetting how to study, and no longer go to Seneca or to Cicero or to Blake to fortify their character.

Dahlberg has also revived an Elizabethan literary form. *Because I Was Flesh* is doubtless an autobiography, but Dahlberg's work extends far beyond the modern limits of that form. Instead of the flat stylistic tedium and the imposing egoism which dominate so many of our American efforts in this field, Dahlberg has given us the celerity and shrewd insights that we associate with fiction. In this book Dahlberg has re-introduced us to the Elizabethan "true-report" and he has managed to overcome the dreariness of modern biographical writing.

In renouncing *Bottom Dogs* and turning to the methods in *Because I Was Flesh*, Dahlberg has shown a spiritual and literary maturity almost lost to American writing. Dahlberg has tried to draw us out of our languor in our literary excrement, and he has come to realize that the villainy and ignominy which dominate our novels indicate only that we are philistines. If we do not heed his wisdom and if, like the Yahoos, we continue to delight in our own filth, we cannot expect anything but ill.

The primary sin of the modern critic of literature is sloth. Instead of attempting the sustained effort necessary to lead men from

143

folly and error, he often adopts a utilitarian morality and, like a Judas goat, steers a dubious course to false knowledge. For such a man it is easier to see literature simply as an historical process, to view the creative act as a scientific attempt to verbalize "class consciousness," and to succumb to the monetary measure of success. The mind of this fraudulent seer becomes bound by pernicious chronology and empty scientism, and he loses the ability to distinguish the truth.

Our modern critics have become so absorbed with the literary trivia of the stylish academics that they have lost sight of the basic nature of critical involvement. Allen Tate has explained:

> The act of criticism is analogous to the peripety of tragedy; it is a crisis of recognition always, and at times also of reversal, in which the whole person is involved.

Not enough men in endowed chairs in literature will admit this, and some of those who do are too withered to make virile judgements.

It has been too easy to use the gadgets of sociologists and polemicists who disguise themselves as patrons of letters. It has been too easy for our writers to renounce the greatest writings of world literature as impotent in the modern age. It has been too easy to abjure the act of human judgement and to let financial success be an index of quality. The modern reader has been led away from the best in literature, and when he approaches a great work his thinking has been directed by scientific critics.

Edward Dahlberg has attacked all these tendencies in modern criticism. He has assailed the literary puppets and social animals who seek only wealth and deny the toil of the honest critic or writer. He has no use for those literary arbiters who offer Trimalchian hospitality to the modern scribbler and who bask in the comfort of undeserved repute. He demands less concern for wealth and position and more for the honest artisan:

> Ibsen said that what is important is not to define literature but to oppose those who are against it. The greatest foes of poems and novels are those in the elite writing business: the Sunday news-

paper book editors and the preposition and adjective friars of the universities. The former hawk books as if they were goods, the latter as if they were parts of speech. The text and the gospel of each is FOR SALE.

Dahlberg has reviled the cult of Lucre and he has rebuked the charlatans and literary demagogues who deceive the public and themselves with false judgements and feigned expertise.

Dahlberg has also shown us the malady of our own writing which acknowledges no tradition, and which, in its search for the unique, has bartered its literary heritage for the lentils of celebrity. How many of our writers are too concerned with their own precious originality to remember that all truly great writing has an over-riding obligation to truth and beauty? How many have eschewed the great traditions in world literature to study the petty scribblings of their fellows? It is these Dahlberg castigates when he bemoans our lack of literary awareness:

> Every time shoaly doggerel is praised pensive verse is lost. How tiresome are the canting chimes of our pedantic journals on Henry James, Pound, Eliot, Lawrence, Gertrude Stein, and Hemingway. One might imagine there had never been such figures as Theophrastus, Porphyry, Plotinus, Clement of Alexandria, Gavin Douglas, Samuel Daniel, Owen Felltham or La Bruyere. Who refers to Dekker's *Plague Pamphlets*? As one French critic said: "You can't find eight professional writers who have read Voltaire."

Dahlberg demands that we return to the greatest in world literature for the wisdom to write our own. For him the tradition T. S. Eliot wrote of has been too long neglected while we have preened our individual talents. Dahlberg has not simply written an essay acknowledging the existence of such traditions and their importance; he has revealed and enriched them with every sentence from his pen.

Finally, Dahlberg has attacked the cumbersome accretion of sham opinion which has developed around great literature. This Stygian accumulation of jargon-filled criticism has ever been Dahlberg's target, and his battle cry has been:

So let us have done with the quackery of drab relativism . . .
Away with the scientific, the psychoanalytic and the proletarian
fraud in literature. Enough of the maundering truisms on poems
and artists from the Poloniuses upon the Hamlets, from the
Jungs, the Otto Ranks, the Plekhanovs, the Trotskys, the Marxists. Enough of this man is split, that poet is mad, and that novelist is class-conscious. What need had the artist to make himself
whole, were he not split?

Dahlberg has revealed the bases for the false authority by which
our modern readers have been deceived. Through our presumptuous
determination to dissect great literature with the scalpels of science,
we have assured ourselves of nothing more than our own ignorance.

If Dahlberg will have none of the slick judgements of editorial
and academic fools, the fashionable writing of the unlettered moderns, and the spurious scientism of the Freudians and Marxists,
what kind of criticism does he demand? In *Can These Bones Live*
Dahlberg provides us his standards of the critical act:

> Criticism is an act of creative faith, and there is no historical ap-
> proach that can ultimately disclose mummified secrets, sphinxed
> in time and place, that the naked eyes, the bones and the pulses
> cannot of themselves discover or apprehend. The critic who hides
> behind science is concealing NO-BODY. Criticism, painting,
> poetry, are but deeply awakened self-love. AMOR FATI means to
> love one's fate and truths, and he who does not love his own
> truths, absolutely, would be more truthful if he kept silent.
>
> All is relative, murmurs the poltroon. True! Now that this is
> granted, have we not the right to demand what the critic feels
> and sees, Absolutely, in this tragic, fleeting and relative world?

In demanding that we realize the human significance in the act of
literary criticism, Dahlberg would tear our pusillanimous experts
away from the false security of their scientific and monetary standards. What fewer critics we would have if all had to confront the
act of judgement in the fashion Dahlberg and Tate have described!

In redirecting our attention to the act of personal evaluation,
Dahlberg demonstrates the eclecticism of his critical approach and,

once again, his respect for past critical traditions. In his concern for the unique integrity of the work itself, Dahlberg has adopted some of the standards of the new criticism; but he also realizes that great literature hardly exists in an aesthetic vacuum. On the contrary, Dahlberg has reminded us of the artist's obligation to eternal standards of literary perfection and moral excellence. He has blended two approaches into a viable critical system, and he has recalled for us that good writing has a powerful effect on the soul.

Though the man of genius is almost always an enigma to his contemporaries, it is time to accord Edward Dahlberg the recognition he deserves.

147

Paul Carroll

AN INTRODUCTION TO EDWARD DAHLBERG
"Omne Animale Post Coitu Triste"

FOR HIS PATRICIAN prose that seems to come from another century, his savage and often cantankerous condemnation of most of the masters of modern literature, his handling of the old myths as if Agamemnon or Quetzalcoatl or the Sorrowful Mother were our real contemporaries, and his sibylline call to abandon our civilization lock, stock and barrel and return to an Arcady of "the sheepcote, the threshing-floor, and the augur's timbrel," Edward Dahlberg has become one of the scandals of American Letters, although a distinguished one. He is one of our own. Yet his stance appears so absolute and odd that anyone with a conventionally solid knowledge of American literary traditions can be disarmed or exasperated when first exposed to it. The first time I saw the stance and heard Dahlberg talk I was astounded. During the winter of 1958 the poet Isabella Gardner gave a party for him at the Cliff Dwellers Club in Chicago. Miscellaneous poets, book reviewers, English professors, and other members of the local intellectual community sat over cocktails, many of us aghast as Dahlberg—tall, dressed in Harris Tweed and silk foulard ascot, handsome with white hair and trim, regimental mustache—fascinated and outraged by his high, bitter invective against most of the idols of contemporary American writing. What he said about Hemingway, Faulkner, Eliot, Edmund Wilson, Pound, and, I believe, the New Critics was univocal, brilliant, sour, erudite, and unanswerable. Good words were given only to Sherwood Anderson and grudging respect to Dreiser, both of whom Dahlberg had known and respected when he was learning

149

how to write in the New York City of the 1930s. At one point I remember feeling that we were not in the Cliff Dwellers Club overlooking Michigan Avenue but were instead in the study of Robert Burton at Christ Church, Oxford, the late Elizabethan sunlight trickling through the windows, the large, worn calfskin folios of Tertullian, Plotinus, Dionysius of Halicarnassus, Paracelsus, or the gossip Diogenes Laertius within easy reach if the speaker had need to check some recondite allusion to score his point. Only the cadence of his sentences and cultivated accent seemed to keep Dahlberg's words from becoming a scream.

Long one of the heroes of the literary Underground because of his early proletarian novels, his jeremiads, and his elevated conception of the vocation of the writer—for which he has spent most of his 65 years in poverty, lack of "respectable" recognition, the recipient of no major literary award—Dahlberg has also earned the admiration of several of the leading men of letters of the Establishment, some of whom, like Sir Herbert Read, have called him a lord of the language, the heir of Sir Thomas Browne, Burton, and the Milton of the great polemical pamphlets. Still, Dahlberg has passed his literary life as an outcast—an Ishmael come out of the Midwest as if the fertile prairies of his native Missouri were barren as the ancient Thebaid or the wastes around the Mareotic Sea, the home only of scorpion, owl, and Egyptian devils.

II

Certainly there is no prose like Dahlberg's prose in all of American literature. At its best, the Dahlberg style is monumental and astonishing. Decades were spent in its evolution. Limited recognition came early when Dahlberg published the novel *Bottom Dogs* in 1929 with a shrill, chilly introduction by D. H. Lawrence. Two more novels followed—*From Flushing to Calvary* (1932) and *Those Who Perish* (1934)—both written in the hard-bitten, bony, slangy style of *Bottom Dogs,* which the author later discredited. The great Dahlberg style first appeared in the collection of critical essays *Do These Bones Live* (1941), later republished as *Can These Bones Live.* Ten years later *The Flea of Sodom* appeared; the style

150

had become supple, bizarre, a weapon of rage and authority. The flowering was to come in Dahlberg's masterpieces *The Sorrows of Priapus* (1957) and the autobiography *Because I Was Flesh* (1964). What commends this style are the cadence and dignity of its sentences and the rich, queer erudition. What is most memorable is its treatment of myth.

Myth is as natural to Dahlberg's sensibility as air, earth, water, and fire. He never uses myth simply as a literary device; instead he lives myth, experiencing his deepest feelings and life in terms of myths.

In *Because I Was Flesh*, for instance, Dahlberg renders his mother Lizzie, a melancholy but Breughelian peasant grasping at the shards and patches which were her life, as the embodiment of the Sorrowful Mother; at other times as the Magdalene or the sister of Lazarus; and finally, through the strength of his prose, she becomes a kind of myth in her own right. Early in the book he makes this passionate, fanatical confession: "Should I err against her dear relics or trouble her sleep, may no one imagine that she has not always been for me the three Marys of the New Testament. Moreover, what I imagine I know is taken from my mother's body and this is the memoir of her body." To call one's mother the three Marys of the New Testament is either to invite ridicule (which the author never encourages) or to insist on a dimension which could prove a disaster in the hands of a lesser writer. But as the events of Lizzie Dahlberg's life are told—how she abandons a doltish husband and two infants to run away with a dude barber, and how later, alone, she bears Edward in a Boston charity hospital; how she eventually settles in Kansas City, Missouri, where amid shabby respectability, greed, and vice she labors as a lady barber and strives to raise her boy and to acquire a new husband; how rotten luck dogs her as suitor after suitor disappoints her, including the last one, a dotty, stinging, rich merchant named Tobias Emeritch, whose wooing of Lizzie provides one of the high moments of comedy and pathos in our literature; how she dies old and alone, in pain, half-crazed—as these events unfold Lizzie Dahlberg *becomes* the three Marys of the Gospels. She becomes Mary the Virgin Mother in that the author, like Jesus, feels that no man really possessed her but himself; Mary the Magdalene in that a stable of suitors actually copulated with her; and Mary the sister of Lazarus in that the author by conjuring back the ghost of his boyhood is her brother, and during the hobo wanderings of his young manhood he is always dead, like Lazarus, until he returns home to her.

One of the commonplaces of modern criticism tells us that the people of myth are contemporaneous with the present. Tiresias broods in the room of the London typist as she submits to the mechanical seduction of the young man carbuncular in *The Waste Land;* Circe, Aeneas, and Thetis appear, disappear, and appear again in the American Army prison camp among Ezra Pound and his fellow prisoners, Snag and his buddy, and the "little coon" and the "big black nigger" in *The Pisan Cantos.* But Dahlberg possesses that rarer gift of being able to resurrect by means of his prose, which is another thing from having the literary imagination to introduce a mythological person into one's poem or novel, or from having the talent to create a memorable fictional character or to write good biography about someone dead. Finding in the events of Lizzie Dahlberg's life echos of the three Marys resurrects these dead women. Much like Odysseus slaughtering sheep to provide blood for the shades in the Cimmerian Underworld, Dahlberg seems to offer the Marys the blood of his mother, a woman as each of them was before becoming a legend among the faithful or a statue in a cathedral or an abstraction to whom one prays—a woman who bears children with her body, who aches, laughs, weeps, defecates, loves, ages, lusts, who wants "to walk quiet and slow among soft dusk" but who dies in pain. The deeper meanings in the events of Lizzie's biography assume shape through the lives and significances of the three Marys; they, in turn, exist once again through her.

When *Because I Was Flesh* ends with an unforgettable and medieval description of Lizzie Dahlberg's death rattle, suffered in a cold-water flat on East 96th Street in New York City, and the final sentence turns into a scream of eloquence, the final metamorphosis occurs in which Lizzie, like the Marys before her, becomes myth through the mystery of words. "When the image of her comes up on a sudden—just as my bad demons do—and I see again her dyed henna hair, her eyes dwarfed by the electric lights of the Star Lady Barbershop, and the dear, broken wing of her mouth, and when I regard her wild tatters, I know that not even Solomon in his lilied raiment was so glorious as my mother in her rags. Selah."

Another use of myth, especially when sexual feelings are involved, exposes one of the origins of many myths. Recalling one of our most tenacious, infantile fantasies, Dahlberg writes in *Because I Was Flesh*: "Once, at daybreak, he [the boy he was] suddenly awakened, hearing his mother let out a cry of pain. Harry Cohen was covering her, and he knew that the cause of her pain was carnal. The baker was one of the issue of those giants who, in the Ethiopic *Book of Enoch*, were said to have had the monstrous privy members of horses." To be reminded of an esoteric text while describing a Kansas City baker helping to make the beast with two backs, and remain bone-serious about it, could lay open the author to a suspicion of unintentional silliness if it were not for the intimation that one of the darker roots which create and nourish certain myths might lie in our reluctance to face raw, shocking events in our immediate emotional lives. Myth, in this sense, distorts emotional fact by displacing it; and by distorting permits us to retain and live with those facts. Who wants to think directly about his mother engaging in sexual intercourse? If her lover is some giant out of Ethiopia, then he—like the Paraclete who inseminates the Blessed Virgin—comes from another country: he is more fairy tale than human. Transformation of sexual feelings into myths occurs continually throughout Dahlberg's writing and accounts for some of his finest passages.

Can These Bones Live, on the other hand, transforms the books of an entire people into myth. The central, brutal intuition of this reading of classic American literature revolves around a retelling of the myth of Genesis, the Fall, Salvation, and Apocalypse, with one significant variation: the Salvation is perverted. Whereas Whitman becomes "the pioneer Cosmos, before him nothing," and Poe "the Adamic Evil," and *Moby-Dick*, "the allegory of the disincarnate Ahab seeking after his own flesh," the Messiah is the Puritan Christ—the Logos stripped of hair, skin, bone, anus, guts, and

genitals. American literature, Dahlberg declares, is the Doomsday
Book of a people who have never known the body of the Incarnation except as a nightmare of incest, paranoia, homosexuality, fear
and hatred of woman, violence, and masochism. This Doomsday
Book, in fact, is one long, insane epithalamium to the effeminate
Christ without a body. By way of contrast, Dahlberg invokes a
composite, secular figure of Incarnation whom American writing
has failed to create: Don Quixote and Sancho Panza, the spirit
"with windmills in the head," and the body, all good belly and
groin. Although no Salvation or Second Coming can be expected
from the perverted Christ there is an Apocalypse. At the other end
of time the Whore of Babylon appears as the Dynamo of Henry
Adams "that has taken us far underground, where we wander over
flowerless and treeless plains of macadam," inhabited by the shades
of Hemingway, Faulkner, and the proletarian novelists. Despite
the efforts of these writers, in Dahlberg's reading, to resurrect the
body that the Puritans like Poe and Hawthorne and Melville tried
to bury, they are shown as the other side of the same bad coin.
Either they write merely of "the kidney, the prostate gland, and
the intestinal tract," or they catalogue no more than the Drama of
Bread. Apocalypse, in short, is contemporary American literature.

In an America where myths—except the usual chauvinistic type
or those celebrating Herculean muscle or Horatio Alger success—
have seldom been part of how the citizens experience or comprehend realities, Dahlberg is our one mythological poet. During forty
years of writing he has performed the lonely ritual of recalling to
a pragmatic American world, with its chaos and hearty vulgarities,
the fact that men once found grandeur and tragedy in myths that
embodied some of the bedrock realities of this life and of the life of
the imagination.

III

Dahlberg despises contemporary America. In his condemnation of
it, no American writer since Thoreau—with his stubborn Yankee
contempt of the business world, culture, manners, and religion of
the 19th century, which he dismissed as "restless, nervous, bustling,

154

trivial"—has worn the cloak of Diogenes with such conviction, day in and day out, decade after decade. Because of the rigor of Dahlberg's hatred, frequently couched in Old Testament vocabulary and fury, some critics and fellow writers have hailed him as a prophet. He is not. His condemnation is grounded neither on an ancient morality, such as that of Jeremiah or Isaiah, based on the tablets of the law given by the god of their fathers, nor on a new morality, a new delineation of what it could mean to be human, the arrogant, virile transcendence of the old gods called for by the Zarathustra of Nietzsche. Instead, the moral energy with which Dahlberg hurls anathemas at our world comes from a peculiar kind of reverence and from a calendar of literary saints of his own making.

His reverence, rooted more in the heart than in the head, is a reverence for the archetypes from the childhood of the race. Throughout his books and letters Dahlberg bestows an almost religious honor upon the Greek heroes out of Homer, Plutarch, and the tragic and comic poets, and upon the Old Testament patriarchs of the cow pasture, the plain of Sharon, and the cedars of Lebanon. At other times, his piety honors the gods of maize, squash, and rain, the reptile, animal, and bird gods of the Incas, Aztecs, Potowattamies, and the nomad tribes of the Western plains. Invoking these heroes and deities Dahlberg condemns out of hand "this immense mortuary cartel," contemporary America. This is not prophecy. This is piety for the elemental, the primitive, the genesis which is each sunrise; and it is hatred for all that is mechanized and sophisticated which separates men from the natural world. "I think you are potentially right," he writes in a letter to Sherwood Anderson in 1939, "in believing that it is the machine that has rifled man in this country of talk, sexual communication, the human companionable touch. As for myself, I'm a medievalist, a horse and buggy American, a barbarian, anything, that can bring me back to the communal song of labor, sky, star, field, love."

Still at other times, Dahlberg renounces the world and all its pomp by invoking the authority of his literary saints. Villon, Pascal, Poe, Baudelaire, Nietzsche, Dostoyevsky, and, when he is not angry at him, Herman Melville—the names change from time to time but the reason why Dahlberg bestows sanctity remains. Inclusion in the calendar seems to be predicated on three attributes: the man must have written well, suffered in his life, and died before this century began, which was when Dahlberg was born. Contemporary man with his newspaper prose, cars, offices, telephones, income tax returns, and political causes is measured against the lives and works of these saints and found wanting. This is not prophecy. This reflects a search—at times desperate, at times deeply moving—among great dead writers for metaphors with which to present and explain oneself to oneself and to the world; and it is hatred of human follies and virtues which are foreign to one's own nature.

IV

I suggest that Dahlberg's achievement rests primarily in this: he is the Job of American Letters. His lamentation calls not on the god who speaks out of the whirlwind; nor does it call on this American century with its poverty of reverence for the elemental deities. His lamentation is a quarrel with the body—its Sophoclean birth— "never to have been born is best"—its bestialities, maladies, winds, its affronts to the spirit, and most of all, its sexual torpors, its sexual absurdities, its incessant, droning sexual demands.

A certain immemorial quality (which only Melville, among the Americans, has also achieved) pervades this quarrel. It is as if Dahlberg's dialogue with his body could occur in any culture and in any century, as far back perhaps as the origin of man's harsh, sore dialogue with his flesh: "I was naked," Adam said, "and I hid." Sometimes when I am reading Dahlberg I indulge in the reverie that the author, his face half-concealed behind a medieval hood, has stalked the narrow streets "twisted like a sheep's gut" of the Ile de la Cité in the Paris of Abelard, bitter at the spectacle of the dance of flesh and death surrounding him, knowing, too, that he is an actor in it; or I see him standing in the Agora, his sympathies with the sayings and bizarre antics of the Cynics, "the dogs of philosophy," murmuring with approval the famous passage at the beginning of *The Republic* where Plato has old Cephalus say:

"How well I remember the aged poet Sophocles, when in answer to the question, How does love suit with age, Sophocles—are you still the man you were? Peace, he replied, most gladly have I escaped the thing of which you speak: I feel as if I had escaped from an insane and furious master."

What strikes the unmistakably indigenous American note about Dahlberg's dialogue with the body is that he never celebrates or documents the ecstasies or even the animal delights of the flesh. In *The Sorrows of Priapus* and *Because I Was Flesh* the body is put on trial, prosecuted with a sustained rage and occasionally with droll, acidic wit, as in this passage in which Dahlberg gives clear statement to his central theme—man's old bafflement over the daemon of his own sexuality.

> The penis, despite the fact that it is attached to each person, has its own disposition; it goes where it will, and though the spurious owner wants to think, it wants to urinate, and if its helpless landlord desires to read or to sow grass it wants to lie in bed . . . A man may want to study Mark, or Paracelsus, or go on an errand to do a kindness to an aged woman, but this tyrant wants to discharge itself either because the etesian gales are acerb or a wench has just stooped over to gather her laundry. The whole matter, when one thinks of it reasonably, is bizarre. The head is so obtuse as to go absolutely crazy over a pair of hunkers, which is no more than a chine of beef.

To say that Dahlberg's central theme consists in a prosecution and an exorcism of the body is only to suggest that despite his classical and biblical allusions and the gorgeous, Elizabethan vocabulary, he works at the core of one of the most persistent traditions in American writing—a tradition which he was among the first to define. I allude to the tradition of the morning after the Fall into sexual consciousness: the body, now the adversary, is viewed with suspicion, anger, contempt; violence against the female or against oneself often erupts; the cultivation of an exacerbated state of frustration usually begins. *Omne animale post coitu triste*: this melancholy dogma informs the American classics from the *Tales* of Edgar Allan Poe, *The Scarlet Letter*, *Moby-Dick*, *An American*

Tragedy, Winesburg, Ohio, The Sun Also Rises to contemporary
novels like William Burroughs' *Naked Lunch* and Norman
Mailer's *An American Dream*. How deeply rooted this tradition is
may be seen by looking at the other side of the same mirror. There
we witness that longing for a lost bucolic summer world: the days
of Huckleberry Finn upon the raft, Nick Adams hunting and fish-
ing in Northern Michigan, the winter nostalgia of Holden Caul-
field for the ducks of Central Park, the bumptious exuberance of
Jack Kerouac and his buddies in *On the Road*: an Eden where the
adolescent boy forever retains his purity and sexual innocence.
Few American writers worth their salt have not contributed to this
tradition, and in this tradition Dahlberg is one of the masters. In
Edward Dahlberg we have a classic on our own back porch. One
reads him at one's peril. At its best his prose asks nothing less than
Cardinal Newman's motto: *cor ad cor loquitor*, "heart speaketh to
heart."

158

KAY BOYLE

A MAN IN THE WILDERNESS

IN A LETTER written in 1958 from Mallorca, Spain, to William Carlos Williams in Rutherford, N. J., Edward Dahlberg cries out in despair: "As soon as you have architecture anywhere today you have foolish opinionated buildings, dogmatic functionalism, and all the depravity of the up-to-date, inhuman city. Nobody is educated enough any more to build a simple, unaffected home which is good, and has as much feeling, as an ancient proverb. When I look at a motorcycle or a taxi there are tears in my heart. For all the earth is ours, our habitation and sepulcher, and every country that falls under the infamy of money is a terrible wound to every other people."

Writing to Lewis Mumford from Berkeley, California, in 1953, Dahlberg reproaches Mumford for his worship of the machine, and cautions him that to see "beauty in machinery is a great perversity," unworthy of his nature. In New York in 1951, Dahlberg writes his friend, Sir Herbert Read, that he does not approve of his way of living. "Do you think it is good to go to the foes of art to heal the artist? I don't care what money you get for whom, what you are doing is at the bottom a sin." He warns Read that he lives too shrewdly, and that this is "the worst error of a poet." For man must thirst, and must remain in the company of those who are athirst, he writes; and even if solitude is "a great pain in the heart," still "a man must remain in the wilderness."

To read Dahlberg's two present collections, *Epitaphs of Our Times*, his letters, and *The Edward Dahlberg Reader*, is to enter that wilderness and to be all but overwhelmed by his passionate

159

chronicling of the unremitting affront to the spirit which makes alienation the greatest peril to contemporary, sensitive man. The loneliness and the separateness which result from this affront are apt to engender a climate favorable to art. Kafka wrote of the consequences of disesteem obliquely, his language German, his vehicle allegory, and startled the lost to a deeper recognition of how forsaken they were. Dahlberg, whose work may be compared to Kafka's in its intensity of discernment and foreboding, writes of that merciless assault on the spirit in cadenced, occasionally archaic and consistently splendid English. His language is classic, his metaphor frequently myth, but both language and myth belong to him alone.

Kafka was, in his time, not only Germany's most disturbing but most reliable prophet. As an artist, he foretold with the maddest courage all the horror that was to come. Dahlberg, whose more than a dozen remarkable books have established a unique reputation for him in Europe, as well as in America, deserves our recognition not only as stylist, as critic, as poet but also as eloquent and unflinching prophet. He declares against the outrage to every sensibility that faces us at this moment whichever way we turn upon our native soil, and he grieves for the disaster that lies, still undefined, beyond the perilous rim of contemporary American violence. What modern man calls progress, Dahlberg recognizes (with Yeats) as the dying of men's hearts. He sees the degradation of love and learning everywhere.

The ambiguous self in relation to history, to country, to sex, and to eternity, is furiously alive in all of Dahlberg's work, but it is in his letters that that self emerges in all its restless continuity. The letters are pages torn from the annals of his nights and days, his hopes and griefs, and transmuted into the actual substance of compassion, understanding and yearning for those who are for the moment beyond the reach of his hand. "Bill Williams, you know, had another small stroke; I tremble for him, and also weep for him," Dahlberg writes to Josephine Herbst in 1958. "He has done so many things of which I disapprove, but how little I want to go on rebuking him. Poor, poor Bill, he is much too close to Nature. I would kill Nature could I save him."

But despite the sincere passion of his declared love, there is all too often a wariness in his approach to those whom he addresses, a lurking overzealousness that leaves one with the feeling that every human relationship Dahlberg has had was, without exception, a heartbreak to him in the end. At the very moment that he declares himself, he appears to tremble at the prospect of another devastating experience, still another emotional catastrophe from which he will never quite recover. "What the two of you cannot know," he writes to the Allen Tates in 1965, "is that I fear going to other people's homes, and when I do, I leave as fast as I can, without seeming to be rude. It is not that I do not care deeply for my friends, or that I prefer to be with flimsy acquaintances rather than with the aristocratic intellects of our world. I dread unknowable disaster."

Lawrence Durrell once wrote a number of letters to Henry Miller on the subject of the artist's fear of accepting his own identity. He cited to Miller "Cezanne's fear that society would get the grappins on him . . . Gauguin's insistence on what a hell of a fine billiards player he was . . . and D. H. Lawrence fervently knitting, knitting, and trying to forget *Sons and Lovers*"—and there was Miller himself eating like mad to establish a reputation for himself as a gourmet. "Here are numberless types," Durrell wrote, "of the same ambiguous desire on the part of the artist to renounce his destiny. To spit on it." This was not for the moment Dahlberg's desire or dilemma. He knew from the beginning who he was and that he was destined, both as man and writer, to be an exile in the land of his birth. "First in the wanton streets of Kansas City," he writes to William Carlos Williams in 1957, "then in an orphanage, and then a waif of letters in New York." His dilemma, rather, was *how* to be a writer, and he studied the works of others avidly, seeking to find that way.

From the time of the appearance of his first novel, *Bottom Dogs*, published in 1929, there could be no question but that he had found his own exceptional speech. The Job of American letters, one critic has called him; and others have termed his autobiography, *Because I Was Flesh*, a masterpiece, and "one of the few important American books published in our day." "The truth is," this outsized figure of American literature writes almost in panic to his friend Allen Tate (from Mallorca in 1962), "that I am a great coward before I dare venture one sentence. No man goes to the guillotine with greater apprehension than I sit down at my desk, no longer with a quill or a pen, but with a fell machine . . ." For to Dahlberg, a book is "a battle of the soul and not a war of words."

Leon Edel recently took Joyce to task for calling out in his letters for help, love and money. Dahlberg's letters appeal for these same solaces. Is the artist to be reproached for articulating the constant cry of all living men; is he not rather to be cherished for having spoken it so eloquently? And is not the attempt to answer that despairing cry the reason for all teaching, all learning, all writing, from the Greeks to Abelard, from the Old Testament to Joyce?

The voices of Camus and Sartre, Faulkner and Hemingway, no longer reach the young in the far journey they are taking; and Salinger, who was once their spokesman, is now more silent than the tomb. This wayfaring generation, hair long on the shoulders and wounded faces staunched by beards, murmurs of Allen Ginsberg, Timothy Leary and Bob Dylan, uncertain as to whether these saviors (or even William Burroughs and John Rechy) are saying fearlessly and honestly enough the words that must somehow be said. Born in 1900, Dahlberg offers a philosophy of rebellion, but of dignity and discipline as well, to the young who have the insight to look his way. That philosophy, strong and undismayed, is stated in almost every page he writes. It is there in "The Tragedy of American Love" and in "Heart Speaketh to Heart," both of which are included in *The Edward Dahlberg Reader*. It is there in his uncompromising letters, and strikingly there in his essay, "Thoreau vs. Contemporary America," in which he extends his hand to the uneasy, saying:

> We are fatalists only when we cease telling the truth, but, so long as we communicate the truth, we move ourselves, life, history, men. There is no other way. This is the simple epitome of the wisdom of nonresistance to evil. It is what Confucius, Thoreau, and Tolstoi taught. It is the incredible, the visionary way, and it announces treason and betrayal more boldly than firearms or airplanes.

162

A SELECTED BIBLIOGRAPHY
OF EDWARD DAHLBERG

WORKS

1929   *Bottom Dogs*, London: G. P. Putnam's Sons [1929]

1932   *From Flushing to Calvary*, New York: Harcourt, Brace and Company [1932]

1932   *Kentucky Blue Grass Henry Smith* (A separate publication of Part Six of *From Flushing to Calvary*), Cleveland: White Horse Press, 1932.

1934   *Those Who Perish*, New York: John Day Company [1934]

1941   *Do These Bones Live*, New York: Harcourt, Brace and Company [1941]

1947   *Sing O Barren* (A revision of *Do These Bones Live*), London: George Routledge & Sons, 1947.

1950   *The Flea of Sodom*, London: Peter Nevill Limited [1950]

1957   *The Sorrows of Priapus*, [Norfolk, Conn.: New Directions, 1957]

1960   *Can These Bones Live* (A revision of *Do These Bones Live*), New York: New Directions, 1960.

1961   *Truth Is More Sacred*, New York: Horizon Press [1961]

1964   *Because I Was Flesh*, [Norfolk, Conn.] New Directions [1964]

1964   *Alms for Oblivion*, Minneapolis: Univ. of Minnesota Press [1964]

1965   *Reasons of the Heart*, [New York] Horizon Press [1965]

1966   *Cipango's Hinder Door*, Austin: The University of Texas [1966]

1967   *Epitaphs of Our Times*, New York: George Braziller [1967]

1967   *The Edward Dahlberg Reader*, [New York] New Directions [1967]

1967   *The Leafless American*, [Sausalito, Calif.] Roger Beacham [1967]

1968   *The Carnal Myth*, [New York] Weybright and Talley [1968]

GENERAL CRITICISM

Ford, Ford Madox, "The Fate of the Semiclassic," *Forum*, Vol. 98, No. 3 (September 1937), pp. 126–128.

Hassan, Ihab, "The Sorrows of Edward Dahlberg," *The Massachusetts Review*, Vol. 5, No. 3 (Spring 1964), pp. 457–461.

Williams, Jonathan, "Edward Dahlberg's Book of Lazarus," *The Texas Quarterly*, Vol. 6, No. 2 (Summer 1963), pp. 35–49.

BOOK REVIEWS

BOTTOM DOGS   1929
Bookman, June 1930
Books, March 2, 1930 (H. Gregory)
Boston Transcript, April 5, 1930
Nation, April 23, 1930 (F. T. Marsh)
Nation and Atheneum, January 25, 1930 (L. L. Irvine)
New Republic, March 26, 1930 (E. Wilson)
New Statesman, February 8, 1930
New York Times Book Review, April 6, 1930
Saturday Review of Literature, March 22, 1930
Saturday Review of Literature, April 12, 1930
Spectator, January 18, 1930 (V. S. Pritchett)
Springfield Republican, April 13, 1930
Times Literary Supplement, (London) December 5, 1929

BOTTOM DOGS   1961
Nation, March 30, 1964 (A. Karlen)
New Statesman, February 9, 1962 (J. Gross)

FROM FLUSHING TO CALVARY
Books, October 9, 1932
Nation, November 16, 1932 (F. T. Marsh)
New Republic, January 4, 1933 (N. Asch)
New York Times Book Review, October 23, 1932
Saturday Review of Literature, November 5, 1932 (C. Simpson)
Springfield Republican, October 23, 1932

THOSE WHO PERISH
Books, September 9, 1934 (F. T. Marsh)
Books, September 23, 1934 (B. Rascoe)
Boston Transcript, October 13, 1934
New Outlook, October 1934
New Republic, November 21, 1934 (K. Burke)
Saturday Review of Literature, September 22, 1934 (C. R.)
Springfield Republican, October 14, 1934
Survey Graphic, November 1934

DO THESE BONES LIVE
American Mercury, June 1941 (M. M. Colum)
Books, April 13, 1941 (A. Kazin)

164

SELECTED BIBLIOGRAPHY

THE FLEA OF SODOM
  The Freeman, July 2, 1951 (J. Chamberlain)
  The New Yorker, September 30, 1950
  Poetry, January 1951 (E. Roditi)

THE SORROWS OF PRIAPUS
  American Quarterly, Winter, 1958 (J. E. Slate)
  Nation, January 11, 1958 (J. Jones)
  New Leader, June 16, 1958 (W. E. Bohn)
  Poetry, April 1959 (R. Duncan)
  Sewanee Review, Spring, 1958 (H. Read)
  Times Literary Supplement, (London) May 9, 1958

CAN THESE BONES LIVE
  American Scholar, Spring 1961 (S. Burnshaw)
  Library Journal, January 1, 1961 (L. W. Griffin)
  Nation, February 4, 1961 (P. Carroll)
  National Review, December 17, 1960 (G. Wills)
  New Leader, February 13, 1961 (E. Capouya)
  Prairie Schooner, Winter 1961 (V. Lipton)
  Sewanee Review, Spring 1961 (A. Tate)

TRUTH IS MORE SACRED
  Booklist, July 15, 1961
  Commonweal, December 8, 1961 (P. Deasy)
  Critical Quarterly, Summer 1962 (J. B. Beer)
  Guardian, December 15, 1961 (J. Daniel)
  Kirkus, March 1, 1961
  Modern Age, Fall 1961 (R. M. Weaver)
  New York Review of Books, March 19, 1964 (R. W. Flint)
  Prairie Schooner, Winter 1962 (J. Williams)
  Saturday Review, April 8, 1961 (G. Hicks)

BECAUSE I WAS FLESH
  Atlantic, March 1964 (W. Barrett)
  Best Sellers, April 15, 1964 (J. G. Brunner)
  Book Week, March 17, 1964 (A. Pryce-Jones)
  Book Week, May 31, 1964 (R. G. Ross)
  Choice, March 1964
  Christian Century, March 18, 1964
  Harper's, March 1964 (P. Pickrel)
  Harper's, April 1964 (B. DeMott)
  Hudson Review, Summer 1964 (D. Aaron)

165

Library Journal, June 15, 1964 (M. L. Barrett)
Listener, May 27, 1965 (G. Baro)
Nation, March 30, 1964 (A. Karlen)
New Leader, January 18, 1965 (J. R. Mellow)
New Statesman, June 11, 1965 (V. S. Pritchett)
New York Review, March 19, 1964 (R. W. Flint)
New York Times Book Review, March 29, 1964 (F. MacShane)
Observer, May 16, 1965 (J. Gross)
Poetry, March 1965 (R. Howard)
Prairie Schooner, Fall 1964 (L. T. Lemon)
Punch, June 16, 1965 (R. G. Price)
Reporter, August 13, 1964 (A. Kazin)
Saturday Review, March 14, 1964 (E. Capouya)
Sewanee Review, Summer 1964 (P. Carroll)
Southern Review, Spring 1965 (J. Herbst)
Spectator, August 13, 1965 (P. Anderson)
Time, March 20, 1964
Times Literary Supplement, (London) August 19, 1965

ALMS FOR OBLIVION
Choice, November 1964
Criticism, Winter 1966 (W. E. Bezanson)
Library Journal, December 15, 1965 (B. W. Fuson)
New Statesman, June 11, 1965 (V. S. Pritchett)
San Francisco Sunday Chronicle, August 2, 1964 (F. MacShane)
Saturday Review, May 30, 1964 (G. Hicks)
South Atlantic Quarterly, Spring 1965 (R. B. Shuman)
Southern Review, Summer 1967 (F. MacShane)
Times Literary Supplement, (London) August 19, 1965

REASONS OF THE HEART
Booklist, November 15, 1965
Nation, September 12, 1966
New Leader, June 6, 1966 (R. Howard)
New York Review, October 20, 1966 (D. Donoghue)
Southern Review, Summer 1967 (F. MacShane)

CIPANGO'S HINDER DOOR
Choice, January 1967
Nation, September 12, 1966 (F. MacShane)
New Leader, June 6, 1966 (R. Howard)
New York Review, October 20, 1966 (D. Donoghue)
New York Times Book Review, June 19, 1966 (X. J. Kennedy)
Poetry, April 1967 (D. W. Baker)
Southern Review, Summer 1967 (F. MacShane)

SELECTED BIBLIOGRAPHY

EPITAPHS OF OUR TIMES
  Atlantic, February 1967 (O. Handlin)
  Book Week, February 5, 1967 (K. Shapiro)
  Chicago Tribune, February 12, 1967 (H. Mitgang)
  Commonweal, March 31, 1967 (B. Cook)
  Harper's, March 1967 (R. Cook)
  Library Journal, February 1, 1967 (D. B. Schneider)
  National Review, September 19, 1967 (A. Kerrigan)
  New Leader, January 16, 1967 (R. Rosenthal)
  New York Review, August 24, 1967 (R. M. Adams)
  New York Times Book Review, March 5, 1967 (F. MacShane)
  Publisher's Weekly, December 26, 1966 (J. Kitchen)
  World Journal Tribune, February 7, 1967 (A. Pryce-Jones)

THE EDWARD DAHLBERG READER
  Booklist, May 15, 1967
  Chicago Tribune, February 12, 1967 (H. Mitgang)
  Commonweal, March 31, 1967 (B. Cook)
  Kansas City Star, January 29, 1967 (W. French)
  National Review, September 19, 1967 (A. Kerrigan)
  New Leader, January 16, 1967 (R. Rosenthal)
  New York Review, August 24, 1967 (R. M. Adams)
  New York Times Book Review, March 5, 1967 (F. MacShane)
  Newsweek, January 23, 1967 (S. Maloff)

THE LEAFLESS AMERICAN
  Library Journal, June 15, 1967 (D. B. Schneider)
  New York Times Book Review, March 5, 1967 (F. MacShane)

NOTES ON CONTRIBUTORS

HAROLD BILLINGS is Assistant Librarian, The University of Texas at Austin. He edited and introduced Edward Dahlberg's *The Leafless American.*

KAY BOYLE teaches English at San Francisco State College. Author of over 25 books, her most recent are *Collected Poems* and *Nothing Ever Breaks Except the Heart.*

PAUL CARROLL, the poet, is editor of the *Big Table Series* (Follett Publishing Company) and *The Edward Dahlberg Reader.*

JOSEPHINE HERBST is author of many distinguished novels and *New Green World,* a study of the Bartrams, eighteenth-century American naturalists.

ALFRED KAZIN teaches English at the State University of New York at Stony Brook. Among his books are *On Native Grounds* and *Starting Out in the Thirties.*

ROBERT KINDRICK teaches English at Central Missouri State College. He studied under Edward Dahlberg at the University of Missouri at Kansas City.

D. H. LAWRENCE is remembered for his novels, short stories, essays, poems, and paintings. Among his many books are *Sons and Lovers* and *Studies in Classic American Literature.*

VICTOR LIPTON, who lives in New York City, has contributed studies of Anais Nin, John Barth, and others to such publications as *Manas, Prairie Schooner, The Village Voice,* and the *Kenyon Review,* where a previous study of Edward Dahlberg was published in the Autumn 1959 issue.

FRANK MACSHANE is Chairman of the Graduate Writing Division, School of the Arts, Columbia University. He has written several books, among them *The Life and Work of Ford Madox Ford*.

SIR HERBERT READ has written many distinguished books in the fields of art, education, literary criticism, and philosophy, as well as poems and the autobiography *Annals of Innocence and Experience*.

JOSEPH EVANS SLATE teaches English at The University of Texas at Austin. He is author of *William Carlos Williams' Image of America*.

ALLEN TATE teaches English at the University of Minnesota. One of the original Fugitive Poets, he most recently edited *T. S. Eliot: the Man and His Work*.

JONATHAN WILLIAMS, poet and publisher, is presently Scholar-in-Residence, Aspen Institute of Humanistic Studies. Of his many books, *Mahler* and *polycotyledonous poems* are the most recent.

WILLIAM CARLOS WILLIAMS had firmly established his name in American letters prior to his death in 1963. Among his best-known works are *In the American Grain* and the *Paterson* poems.

170

INDEX

INDEX

This book has been designed by William R. Holman
and printed on 60 lb. Weyerhaeuser's Scholar Antique Laid.
The text type is Intertype Waverley, a modern face,
with Eric Gill's Perpetua used for the titling.